A Field Guide to Type 2 Diabetes

The Essential Resource from the Diabetes Experts

American
Diabetes
Association.

Writer, Marie McCarren; *Director, Book Publishing*, Abe Ogden; *Managing Editor*, Greg Guthrie; *Production Manager*, Melissa Sprott; *Composition*, Circle Graphics, Inc.; *Cover Design*, Naylor Design; *Printer*, Victor Graphics.

Printed in the United States of America
3 5 7 9 10 8 6 4 2

The suggestions and information contained in this publication are generally consistent with the Clinical Practice Recommendations and other policies of the American Diabetes Association, but they do not represent the policy or position of the Association or any of its boards or committees. Reasonable steps have been taken to ensure the accuracy of the information presented. However, the American Diabetes Association cannot ensure the safety or efficacy of any product or service described in this publication. Individuals are advised to consult a physician or other appropriate health care professional before undertaking any diet or exercise program or taking any medication referred to in this publication. Professionals must use and apply their own professional judgment, experience, and training and should not rely solely on the information contained in this publication before prescribing any diet, exercise, or medication. The American Diabetes Association—its officers, directors, employees, volunteers, and members—assumes no responsibility or liability for personal or other injury, loss, or damage that may result from the suggestions or information in this publication.

♾ The paper in this publication meets the requirements of the ANSI Standard Z39.48-1992 (permanence of paper).

ADA titles may be purchased for business or promotional use or for special sales. To purchase more than 50 copies of this book at a discount, or for custom editions of this book with your logo, contact the American Diabetes Association at the address below, at booksales@diabetes.org, or by calling 703-299-2046.

American Diabetes Association
1701 North Beauregard Street
Alexandria, Virginia 22311

Contents

Acknowledgments v

Introduction vii

1 Biology of Type 2 Diabetes 1

2 Goals of Treatment: Blood Glucose,
   Blood Pressure, Lipids. 19

3 Blood Glucose Monitoring:
   When, Why, How 31

4 Oral Medications. 47

   >> Focus On: What About Diet and
   Exercise Alone? 63

5 Meal Planning 77

>> Focus On: Treatment
of Obesity 110

6 The Power of Movement 121

7 It's Insulin Time 131

8 Too High, Too Low 157

9 Blood Pressure 175

10 Cholesterol 185

11 Your Diabetes Care Team. 195

12 Complications 213

>> Focus On: An Aspirin a Day 226

13 Women 265

14 Kids with Type 2. 277

15 Saving Your Family: Prevention of
Type 2 Diabetes 297

Acknowledgments

For their careful reviews and many helpful comments, we thank David S. Schade, MD; Donald K. Zettervall, RPh, CDE, CDM; Morey W. Haymond, MD; Clara Schneider, MS, RD, RN, LD, CDE; Laurinda Poirier-Solomon, MPH, RN, CDE; Virginia Valentine, CNS, BC-ADM, CDE; and Catherine Gray CNS, BC-ADM, CDE.

A Field Guide to Type 2 Diabetes contains material from case studies and articles that appeared in *Diabetes Forecast, Diabetes Spectrum,* and *Clinical Diabetes*. Contributors include Dennis Gordon, RD, MEd, CDE; Rebecca Murray, APRN, MSN, FNP, CDE; Stephen Podolsky, MD; Neil M.

Scheffler, DPM; Suzanne Boyer, MD; Vishesh Kapur, MD; Julia Warsham, RN; Jan Wall, RD; Kathy Riordan, RN; Donna Hemphill, RN; Carol Randolph, RN; Vivian Fonseca, MD; Anthony N. Fabricatore, PhD; and Thomas A. Wadden, PhD.

Introduction

"Your sugar is high," says your doctor. "You have diabetes."

At the same appointment, your doctor may also have told you, "You have high blood pressure. And your cholesterol levels need work."

High blood sugar, high blood pressure, and unhealthy cholesterol levels so often occur together that the combo has its own name: the metabolic syndrome.

The metabolic syndrome is sneaky. High

You have the **metabolic syndrome** if you have three or more of the following:

- increased waist circumference: over 40 inches for men, over 35 inches for women
- high triglycerides: 150 mg/dl or higher
- low HDL ("good") cholesterol: less than 40 mg/dl in men, less than 50 mg/dl in women
- high blood pressure: 130/85 or higher
- impaired fasting glucose: 100 mg/dl or higher

blood pressure usually causes no symptoms. Unhealthy cholesterol levels don't make you feel bad. The symptoms of high blood sugars are often subtle: "I feel a little tired these days. Probably just getting old . . ."

But over time, the threesome gangs up and puts you at risk for a host of problems: heart attack, stroke, kidney disease, eye problems, and foot ulcers leading to amputation.

Of the three parts of the metabolic syndrome, diabetes is probably uppermost in your mind right now, and most of this book is devoted to helping you control your blood sugars. The bonus is that many of the steps you take to get your blood sugars back in line will also improve your blood pressure and cholesterol levels.

By taking medications your doctor prescribes, eating a healthy diet, being physically active every day, and losing a little excess weight, you can control your blood sugar, blood pressure, and cholesterol. You'll feel better, and you'll add years to your life.

1

Biology of Type 2 Diabetes

You've been diagnosed with diabetes because a blood test showed that you have too much glucose, a type of sugar, in your blood.

This might lead you to believe that glucose is bad. It's not.

Glucose is your body's favorite source of energy. Your muscle and fat cells prefer glucose. And you need to have a certain amount of glucose in your blood to keep your brain working its best.

But too much glucose is a problem. It makes you feel tired. And many years of higher-than-normal levels of glucose lead to the complica-

WHAT IS DIABETES?

Diabetes is a group of diseases in which there is too much glucose (a kind of sugar) in the blood. Today, many types of diabetes are known. The three most common forms of the disease are:

Type 2 diabetes. People with type 2 diabetes can use oral medications, meal planning, weight loss, physical activity, and insulin to control their disease. Most cases of diabetes are type 2 diabetes.

Gestational diabetes. Diabetes that is first diagnosed during pregnancy. In a small number of cases, it is type 1 diabetes that happens to be diagnosed during pregnancy. More commonly, gestational diabetes springs from insulin resistance, which gets worse as the pregnancy progresses. This type is typically diagnosed with a routine blood test at 24 to 28 weeks gestation, and disappears after delivery. It's like temporary type 2 diabetes. It's controlled with meal planning, exercise, and, in some cases, insulin. Women who develop gestational diabetes are at high risk for developing type 2 diabetes later in life.

Type 1 diabetes. The body's immune system has destroyed the insulin-producing cells of the pancreas. People with type 1 diabetes must take insulin to live. Type 1 diabetes affects less than 10% of all people with diabetes.

tions of diabetes: kidney disease, diabetic eye disease, and nerve problems.

So your goal is to keep your glucose levels in the healthy range. To that end, your doctor has probably written you a prescription for medication, said something about "dieting," and mentioned exercise.

When you know what's going on in your body, you'll see how each part of your treatment plan works to make you feel better today, and be healthier for years to come.

Glucose: Two Sources

Food

When you eat, the starches and sugars from the meal are broken down into glucose, a type of sugar. The glucose moves from your digestive tract into your bloodstream.

Your muscle and fat cells want that glucose. But it can't just float into the cells. It needs help to move from your bloodstream into the muscle and fat cells.

The helping hand is insulin, a hormone produced in the beta cells of your pancreas.

Before you developed diabetes, your pancreas was working well. It produced enough insulin for your needs. And your body responded well to insulin. That is, it was sensitive to insulin.

So when you ate, your pancreas detected a rise in blood glucose and responded by secreting a surge of insulin, and your cells would rapidly take in the glucose from the meal. Your blood glucose levels did not go above 140 mg/dl after meals.

Your Liver

Food is not the only source of glucose in the bloodstream. Your liver stores glucose. If you go without food for a long time, such as overnight, your liver releases these emergency stores of glucose.

You don't want your liver to release glucose until you really need it. Insulin signals the liver to hang on to its glucose. So you need a low level of insulin in your bloodstream all day long. Otherwise, your liver would release glucose and your blood glucose levels would go too high.

Before you developed diabetes, your liver responded well to insulin. Just a little insulin would be enough to remind the liver not to release glucose. Overnight and between meals, your blood glucose levels stayed in the range of 70–110 mg/dl.

A Problem Begins

Insulin: High
Glucose: Normal

At some point, your body became less sensitive to insulin. Your muscle and fat cells required more insulin to move glucose in. Your liver needed more insulin as a signal not to release glucose. You had become "insulin resistant."

Your pancreas rose to the challenge and made more insulin. You had high levels of insulin in your blood—perhaps three times higher than people who are not insulin resistant. Doctors call this "hyperinsulinemia." It was enough to overcome your body's resistance to insulin. Your blood glucose levels stayed in the normal range, so you didn't have diabetes yet.

Why did you become insulin resistant? It's partly genetic, partly your environment. You inherited a tendency towards insulin resistance. Then, if you're like many Americans, you gained weight as you got older. Excess weight, especially around your middle, contributes to insulin resistance. And again like most Americans, you probably became less active as you got older. Being sedentary also contributes to insulin resistance. So your genes laid the foundation; your lifestyle built the rest.

Insulin: High
Glucose: Not Always Normal

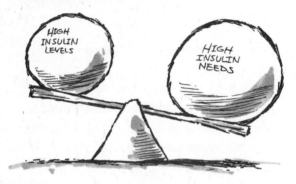

Over time, your insulin resistance got worse. Some people get more and more insulin resistant but are able to produce more and more insulin, so they never develop diabetes.

But you have a second problem. In addition being insulin resistant, you have a defect in your pancreas. It has a limit as to how much insulin it can produce. This usually gets worse as you age.

So after a time of hyperinsulinemia and normal blood glucose levels, your pancreas could not always rise to the challenge. At first, it was sluggish in responding to the glucose from a meal with a lot of carbohydrate (starch and sugar). Your blood glucose levels after a big meal went above 140 mg/dl. You had impaired glucose tolerance (IGT).

As time went on, your pancreas didn't produce enough insulin to keep your liver in check. You had high blood glucose first thing in the morning, over 100 mg/dl, even though you hadn't eaten for eight or ten hours. You had impaired fasting glucose (IFG).

IGT and IFG are both known as pre-diabetes.

Blood tests could have revealed these abnormal glucose levels, but if you're like most people, you didn't have these tests, and you didn't know anything was wrong.

Glucose: High Most of the Time

You aged. Maybe you gained more weight or became more sedentary, so your insulin resistance got worse. Or maybe your pancreas began to produce less and less insulin. Your blood glucose levels were high most of the time. They were over 126 mg/dl before breakfast, they were over 200 mg/dl after meals, or both. You had developed diabetes.

Diagnosis

If you were lucky, you were diagnosed soon after you developed diabetes.

More likely, you had high blood glucose levels for a number of years, and they kept getting higher. You felt dragged out. Maybe you began to get up in the middle of the night to go to the bathroom. You may not have realized you were sick. You may have thought, "It's just age."

On average, people have type 2 diabetes for *eight to ten years* before being diagnosed.

Years of undiagnosed and untreated diabetes take a toll. High blood glucose leads to the complications of diabetes: kidney damage, diabetic eye disease, and nerve damage. In one large study, half the participants already had complications by the time they were diagnosed with type 2 diabetes. You may have shown signs of a developing complication, and that prompted your doctor to test for diabetes.

Treatment

Fortunately, you have now been diagnosed and have started treatment. You'll do best with a treatment plan that addresses all the problems that may be con-

IS IT REALLY TYPE 2?

Most cases of type 1 diabetes are diagnosed in people under age 30. In children, the symptoms of type 1 seem to develop over a few weeks, and the child typically feels very sick.

But sometimes older adults develop type 1. Symptoms come on more gradually than they do in children. The person may feel tired and be drinking more water for months before finally going to the doctor.

So, you're over 40, and your sugars are high. Is it type 1 or type 2? The answer is important. If it's type 2, diabetes pills will probably work well for you. If it's type 1, pills may seem to help in the beginning, but you really need insulin.

Type 2 is more likely if you

- are over 50 years old
- are overweight
- are gaining or maintaining your weight when your glucose is first found to be high
- have several relatives with type 2 diabetes

Adult-onset type 1, also called latent auto-immune diabetes of adulthood (LADA), should be considered if you

- are under 50 years old
- are slender
- are losing weight
- have no relatives known to have type 2

Table 1-1. Criteria for Diagnosis of Diabetes (mg/dl)

	Normal, nondiabetic	Pre-diabetes	Diabetes (A positive test must be confirmed with the same or another test on another day.)
Fasting plasma glucose (Fasting means no caloric intake for at least 8 hours.)	Less than 100	100–125 Impaired Fasting Glucose (IFG)	126 or higher
Blood glucose level 2 hours after drinking a set amount of glucose	Less than 140	140–199 Impaired Glucose Tolerance (IGT)	200 or higher
Random blood glucose (any time of day)			200 or higher, plus symptoms of diabetes (urinating a lot, thirsty, unexplained weight loss)

tributing to your high blood sugars.

Special Case: Very High Glucose

Maybe you were in the minority and had extremely high blood glucose levels—400, 600, or even higher—when you were diagnosed. Here's what might have happened:

For three or five or ten years, you were unaware that your blood glucose levels were higher than normal. Then you had a major stressor in your life. This could have been a major physical stress such as a heart attack, or a major emotional stress.

When your body is under stress, your liver floods your bloodstream with glucose. If you didn't have diabetes, this would be a good thing. This extra glucose would be used to give the body energy to deal with the stress, be it to fight off an infection or run from danger.

But at this point, you did have diabetes. Your liver threw out that extra glucose, but your muscles couldn't take it in because they were insulin resistant, and your beta cells couldn't make enough insulin to overcome this resistance. Your blood glucose went up to 400, maybe 500.

Such levels of blood glucose are toxic. Your beta cells were suffocated by the extra glucose, and they shut down. This **glucose toxicity** may also have made your insulin resistance worse.

Table 1-2. Plan for Normal Blood Sugar Levels

	Oral Medications	Meal Planning	Weight Loss	Physical Activity	Insulin Injections
	Chapter 4	Chapter 5	Chapter 5	Chapter 6	Chapter 7
Your muscle and fat cells are insulin resistant.	✓		✓	✓	
Your pancreas doesn't produce enough insulin.	✓				✓
Your pancreas doesn't respond quickly after a meal.	✓	✓			✓
Your liver releases glucose when it's not needed.	✓		✓		

Your body was now making almost no insulin. Your blood glucose levels shot up even higher. You were very ill. You may have been brought to a hospital.

The appropriate treatment at this point is insulin by injection or in I.V. fluids. This brought your blood glucose down right away.

You were then probably sent home with instructions to continue giving yourself insulin by injection. After a few weeks of insulin treatment, which is the most effective treatment for bringing down blood glucose, your beta cells recovered from their bout with toxic levels of glucose. They came coughing back to life and started to produce insulin again. You needed less and less injected insulin.

You may have then been switched to a more typical diabetes regimen of oral agents, meal planning, and increased physical activity.

FORUM

Throughout this book, you'll find excerpts from the Community Forums found on the American Diabetes Association's Web site. To read or join discussions, go to: www.diabetes.org, click on Message Boards on the top navigation bar. Please note the American Diabetes Association does not review all information shared in the Forum area for accuracy. Those who use the Forum Area are strongly advised to consult their health care professional before altering any treatment.

Diagnosed

I am in total shock. What do I do now? Empty my freezer? There has been no warning for the diagnosis. I feel like I've been given the death sentence although I KNOW this can be handled and controlled. The choice is mine. I am female, 61 years, alone—can you help me get into this?—bth

Re: Diagnosed
Don't empty your freezer—just eat what is in it SLOWER! I was 50 when diagnosed and also shocked. That was 1 day before a 2-week vacation and it scared me

so bad that I LOST 3 lbs during that vacation—was afraid to eat TOO MUCH. After that, I started counting carbs and have about 100 per day (the average person has 300 per day). Also try to exercise all I can (biking, swimming, walking) to burn that sugar. Have kept off meds so far but last A1C was 7.4 so don't know how long I can stave off drugs. Keep your chin up. It is not the end of the world. I can only manage ONE MEAL AT A TIME mentally. But when the meal is over I carry on with my day and forget that I couldn't pig out at the previous meal. Looking in the mirror at a THIN ME is quite a bit of motivation. You are not alone. Be thankful that you didn't get it as a much younger person. Try to look at the positives. Best of luck to you. There is much info here on the internet so educate yourself and DON'T PANIC. It will become a way of life and you will reach acceptance. God bless you. E me if you would like to. —D11

Re: Diagnosed

Shock, anger, denial, the normal reactions to anything that affects your life. It is probably more stressful than marriage, divorce, and just below death of a loved one. It is NOT a death sentence, we all will die for some reason or other. You CAN LIVE for decades with diabetes (latest Diabetes Forecast lead article has had diabetes for 80 years). When your diet is set up with your Dietitian (make sure they are diabetic certified) and doctor medications (they can change over the first 6 months) until you are regulated. You will feel better and do better, it is a diet plan, just like any basic diet plan but it is designed to prevent problems and to provide a better life. Just take care of your feet and maintain the best that you can. I was diagnosed 1/22, so I am recent to this. I am eating well, 3 meals, 3 snacks. Don't skip breakfast or any other meal. Life is no shorter under diabetes if you respect what it means. I am doing much better now than before I knew I had it, and didn't take care of myself so much. Keep your chin up, and smile. —dm

Re: Diagnosed

Thanks soooo much. I am seeing the Dietitian today and will have diabetic counseling next week. I'm not being "good" yet, but will when I have enough information. Then it's pounds off and exercise. I KNOW this is a good thing, but would have preferred having the choice. —bth

Recently Diagnosed

I was diagnosed with Type 2 at the end of January this year. I have been in and out of Dr's appointments since then but am still so overwhelmed with it all. It took me two weeks to break down and cry about it, and that was only because the Drs kept telling me if I didn't get this under control then they would end up having to cut off my feet when complications set in. Even with the scare tactics I'm still having trouble keeping to the diet they put me on—6 meals a day, carbs and proteins each time. I exercise each day, at least 30 minutes on the bike and yes the weight is coming off but I sit and wonder why me? I get angry because of the diabetes and am finding it hard to get a handle on, for the Drs and my family I'm doing great but inside I'm a mess. I feel like at the moment I'm not in control of me and I'm not handling this I'm just putting on a great front for everyone else. I'm sorry that this is a jumble of thoughts, it's the first time that I feel able to say that life [stinks] about now and not be admonished for saying it. Any advice would be appreciated. —E

Re: Recently Diagnosed

I too have been recently diagnosed. The day my life changed, April 26th 10:12am when I got the call from my Drs. office. My wife had to pick me up off the floor. I have children, an ill mother, a loving caring wife. They all depend on me. You too have a host of people that depend on you. Resist the temptation to dwell on the negatives. You have had your eyes opened to a life now that requires your every attention, every thought, every feeling to help you move forward beyond this affliction. Keep working, keeping testing, keep praying, keeping moving forward. People that love you need you. You'll be ok. If you don't like your Drs. Fire them, find ones you like, join your local ADA chapter, keep posting here. I talk to everyone I can, sharing, learning. You'll be ok. —BLK

CHAPTER

2

Goals of Treatment: Blood Glucose, Blood Pressure, Lipids

Diabetes is one part of your metabolic syndrome. The other parts are high blood pressure and unhealthy cholesterol levels.

Controlling blood glucose, blood pressure, and cholesterol will lower your risk of diabetes complications.

Blood Glucose

The United Kingdom Prospective Diabetes Study (UKPDS), the largest and longest study of complications in people with type 2 diabetes, showed that keeping blood glucose levels close to the normal, nondiabetic level reduces the risk of:

- retinopathy (diabetic eye disease, which can lead to vision loss)
- nephropathy (kidney disease)
- possibly neuropathy (nerve problems caused by diabetes)

There are two types of tests that will tell you what your blood glucose levels are. One is the blood glucose checks you do yourself, with your home monitor.

The goals for most nonpregnant adults are below. Your doctor might set different goals for you, depending on your age and your other medical conditions.

Plasma Glucose	Goal
Before meals	90–130 mg/dl
1 to 2 hours after meals	Less than 180 mg/dl

Your Blood Glucose Batting Average: A1C

The checks you do at home may not give you the whole story. Let's say that your fasting blood glucose level is fine, but your blood glucose level goes too high after meals. If you check your blood glucose only before breakfast, you'll think that you're reaching your goals.

If you checked your blood glucose eight or ten times a day, you'd get a truer picture of the real average. But who wants to do that?

There's a blood test that gives you your true average. It tells you how well your diabetes regimen is working. It's called a hemoglobin A1C test (A-one-C). It's like having a hundred glucose checks every day averaged out for you. Here's how it works:

There's always some glucose in your blood. The same is true of people who don't have diabetes.

Glucose links up with the hemoglobin in your red blood cells. If you have a lot of glucose in your blood, more of your hemoglobin will have glucose attached. Once the glucose is attached, it's there for the life of that red blood cell—at most, 120 days.

The percentage of your hemoglobin that has glucose attached can be measured with a blood test done by a lab. In a person who doesn't have diabetes, about 5% of the hemoglobin is "glycated" (has glucose attached). In people who have diabetes, the percentage is higher. How much higher depends on blood glucose levels. An A1C test shows you your average blood glucose level over the previous two to three months. Some call it your blood glucose batting average.

A1C (percent)	Average Plasma Glucose Level (mg/dl)
6	135
7	170
8	205
9	240
10	275
11	310
12	345

(If your lab does a different type of glycated hemo-globin test, the percentages/blood glucose values will be different from those above.)

The goal for most nonpregnant adults is an **A1C under 7%**. If you are pregnant or trying to conceive, the goal is an A1C within the normal range (at many labs, under 6%).

The UKPDS showed that reducing your A1C by 1 percentage point (for example, from 9% to 8%) reduces your risk of retinopathy, nephropathy, and possibly neuropathy by 35%, and reduces the risk of diabetes-related death by 25%.

How Often?

	Have A1C tests:
Your glucose control is stable and you're satisfied with it	Every 6 months
Your treatment plan has changed or you're not meeting your goals	Every 3 months
You're pregnant or trying to conceive	Every 4 to 6 weeks

Most people have their A1C tests done at their doctor's. Several companies market A1C kits to consumers. You take a fingerstick sample and mail it to the lab. You can also get a blood glucose monitor that also tests for a glycated protein, which tells you your average blood glucose level over the previous two weeks. See the American Diabetes Association Resource Guide for information on current products.

YOUR ABCs: KNOW 'EM, CONTROL 'EM

You'll be healthier and live longer if you know
and control your ABCs:

A1C: below 7%

Blood pressure: below 130/80

Cholesterol: LDL under 100 mg/dl

Blood Pressure

The UKPDS showed that lowering blood
pressure reduces the risk of

- stroke
- diabetes-related deaths
- heart failure
- kidney disease
- retinopathy and vision loss

Your goal for blood pressure is:

- under 130/80

You'll find out how to control your blood
pressure in Chapter 9.

Cholesterol

People often talk of their "cholesterol" levels. Doctors call them "lipids." Getting your lipids into the healthy ranges reduces your risk of heart attack (the leading killer of people with type 2 diabetes), stroke, and amputation.

Type of Lipid	Goal
LDL ("bad") cholesterol	Under 100 mg/dl
HDL ("good") cholesterol	Over 40 mg/dl in men, over 50 mg/dl in women
Triglycerides	Under 150 mg/dl

Doing Better!

It's been a month now since my diagnosis . . . saw my doc. on Friday. Labs looking much, much better. Lipids are down and my BS is starting to stabilize (altho' still not as low as I'd like) . . . last night my bedtime BS was 94 . . . first time I've broken 100! But for the most part they're running 105–125. And, the best news of all. . . . I lost 9 pounds!!! For me, that's a biggie (still have 15 or so to go). Life is busy between fingersticks, eating, planning what to eat, exercise, and reading everything about DM I can get my hands on, not much time to panic anymore. I have had one episode of what I believe to be hypoglycemia . . . Really dizzy, weak, sweaty, and sort of disoriented . . . Didn't even think to check my BS . . . but wolfed down a banana, and a peppermint candy I had in my purse (from the old days) . . . felt better in a few minutes and then checked my sugar . . . it was 107 at that point.???? Didn't seem that low, but doc said it probably was low for me right now. All and all, I'm feeling much better. How's it going for you? I'm wondering how everybody out there is getting on . . . You are all a great group . . . it's good to visit now and then . . . Bless you, and take care. —j2

Re: Doing Better!
my A1C came back as 6.0 . . .woooooooooo hooooooooo! I still struggle with getting this planning meals thing down . . . I am making a food diary for the diabetic class I am going to, and I will be seeing the nutritionist in August to get some more help on planning meals and figuring out how to do all this. I have let myself get lazy and I don't cook much. I don't like going out, so I go thru the drive thrus . . . boring. but I need to lose weight really bad and have added the aqua aerobics twice a week. I want to get out and walk and will try to do that each nite. I am glad to hear you are doing better! I have a dumb question tho . . . what are "lipids" and what is DM I assume it is diabetes something? I need to get this new "lingo" down. I figured out what the "bs" was . . . and it is hahaha. take care good to hear from you too! —RP

Re: Doing Better!
I'm sorry, I lapse into "nurse mode" every so

often . . . Lipids are cholesterol, triglycerides, etc. . . . (fat in your blood) . . . DM is "diabetes mellitus" (the official name). Altho' BS could very well describe this disease, I use it for 'blood sugar'. . . you might also see BG (which is blood glucose). Anyway, people with DM also very often have extremely high Lipid levels as I do. . . . Bad thing . . . leads to serious heart trouble. And, by the way, there are no dumb questions. Glad to hear your A1C is so nice and low . . . you must be doing something right. Mine was still 8.3 . . . :-(. . guess it takes a while. (I'm into instant gratification and want everything to be OK immediately) . . . Here's a question for you . . . what do you order when you go to the 'drive thru's'??? I'm so tempted, but am very afraid to do it anymore. For exercise, I bought one of those 'gliders'. . . wonderful machine . . . very low impact and sort of fun. I am up to 2 miles in 35 minutes . . . burns about 250 calories whenever I do it . . . try to do it every day. LOVE IT! We have it set up in front of the TV and the time goes pretty fast. You can work up a sweat . . . or you don't have to. My doc is more impressed with the amount of time I spend on it than the distance I go . . . but, I'm impressed with the distance. You can buy very expensive ones (like from 'Tony Little') or a cheaper variety . . . I bought mine from (believe it or not) QVC. It's called the glider XL. Nice to hear from you and to get the Wonderful news of a low A1C. . . Take care . . . keep in touch. —j2

Re: Doing Better!

Hey, j2! It's good to hear that you're working with the doctor and have a plan going. Nine pounds, eh? I have a foot that weighs nine pounds! Seriously, I have been in touch with my doctor, and I have faxed him my BG readings (ooh, technical talk. . . I love it!) and, as I said earlier, I have a long way to go in the weight-loss department. The good news on that is I have been able to find a couple of plans and articles online, and I have begun to make my meals and calorie intake closely resemble what the plans recommend. In other words, I'm officially on a diet. I want to find out about seeing a nutritionist, and about education classes available to me in the area. The next thing for me is to conquer gravity. It's particularly bad near my couch. Either that, or the sofa's actually possessed. I don't know whether to hire a personal trainer or a priest. I'll let you know. Keep up the good work. It's good to hear some success stories, and it's good to hear from people with good attitudes. —w

3

Blood Glucose Monitoring: When, Why, How

In upcoming chapters, you'll learn how you'll use medication, meal planning, and physical activity to lower your blood sugars.

How will you know that it's all working?

You don't have to go to a lab, give a blood sample, and then wait for your doctor to call with your results. You'll do your own test at home. You'll use a lancet to get a drop of blood from your finger, and your meter will tell you what your blood glucose level is in less than two minutes.

Health care professionals call blood glucose checking "self-monitoring of blood glucose"

(SMBG). It will be a huge help to you and your health care team.

Your doctor will use your blood glucose results to decide whether to up your dose of oral diabetes medication, add another medication, switch you to a different diabetes pill, or add insulin to your regimen.

Your dietitian will use your blood glucose log to design a meal plan for you.

You'll use your blood glucose results to keep yourself motivated to do that simple stroll around the block every day.

When?

When and how often you'll want to check depends on your diabetes plan and whether you're reaching your goals. Your doctor or diabetes educator will suggest a schedule of SMBG for you.

If you've just been diagnosed or just started a new oral medication, your doctor may want you to do SMBG every morning before breakfast, and maybe one other time during the day. You'll report the results to your doctor, who may want to change the dose of medication or try a different one.

Let's say six months later, you've settled on a diabetes plan. You use an oral medication that doesn't cause low blood sugar and you're reaching your goals. Your doctor or diabetes educator may suggest you do SMBG two or three times a week, rotating the times of day. For example, you might check before breakfast two days a week, to get your fasting blood sugar, and then once a week after a meal or before bed.

When you start cutting calories or eating less starch and sugar at meals, you'll want to check before and two hours after some of your meals to see the effect.

If you use insulin, a sulfonylurea, or a glitinide, which can cause your blood sugars to go too low, you'll want to learn the symptoms of low blood sugar and check your blood glucose when you think you're low.

Is that walk or bike ride really doing much for you? Check your blood glucose level afterwards and you'll see that it is!

Write It Down

Don't let your blood glucose results go to waste— write them down. You get a logbook with your first meter. After that, they can be hard to find. Pharmacies may or may not carry them. If you have trouble finding them, ask your diabetes educator, or call the toll-free number for your meter company and ask for more.

If you have complications of diabetes or other medical conditions, you might want to use a spiral-bound notebook instead. You can list more medical information, for example, the blood pressure readings you get at home.

In your logbook, you'll want to record more details about diet and exercise as you're working towards your goals. Once you've settled on a diabetes plan that's working, you can record less detail. Record:

- Day and time of test
- Blood glucose results
- Dose of insulin, if you adjust doses
- What and how much you ate
- How active you were (time, distance)

Bring your log to your medical appointments. You and your doctor or diabetes educator can look for patterns of highs or lows that you can correct.

Blood Glucose Meters

There are over 30 models of blood glucose meter systems. You can find descriptions of them in the Resource Guide, which is updated yearly. All meters perform the basic job of reporting glucose levels in your blood. Some models will suit you better than others. Your diabetes educator can show you several models and help you choose the right one for you. Consider:

- **Sample site and size.** Meters that need smaller-sized blood drops may be easier for those with poor circulation in their hands or who must test in cold environments. Some meters allow you to take samples from the forearm or thigh rather than the fingertip.

■ **Meter size.** Smaller meters slip easily into a shirt pocket when you're on the move. On the other hand, they get lost easily in a deep, dark handbag.

■ **Your dexterity.** If you have trouble with small hand and finger movements, ask your diabetes educator or pharmacist to let you try a few meters before you buy one. Try meters that require less handling or use larger strips. You may also find it easier to use a meter that has strips that come in a vial, rather than individually wrapped in foil. The foil wrappings can be hard to get off.

■ **Timing.** How long are you willing to wait? Some meters take a minute to give results. Some take as little as five seconds.

■ **Your vision.** If you have any trouble seeing or have some degree of color blindness, be sure that you can read the digital display. If you have severe vision loss, make sure that a close companion or family member is trained in the use of your meter so they can help you. For some meters, you can buy a voice synthesizer accessory that talks you through the procedure and results, in English or another language.

■ **Support system.** If you're using a meter for the first time, consider one that offers a video that teaches you how to test. Make sure the company has a 24-hour 800 number to call when you have problems with the meter. Also check that your health care provider is familiar with the model you buy.

▪ **Ease of upkeep.** Each batch of testing strips is slightly different from the last. When you open a new batch, the meter must be calibrated to account for these differences. Then you'll get accurate readings despite tiny differences in strips. Some machines calibrate by themselves. You don't have to do anything with a new batch of strips. On some models, however, procedures can be a little tedious. Some have a two-step procedure using a special strip. Instructions are usually included in every package of strips, so don't panic if you've lost your meter instruction manual.

▪ **Meter memory.** If you have trouble keeping a written log book, select a meter that stores your results in memory. At night you can record the day's readings in your logbook or computer.

Your health care team may prefer you use a certain brand of meter that allows them to connect your meter to their computer and download your readings. Ask your diabetes educator or team member if they do.

If you're comfortable using computers, you can buy software for downloading your results. Each brand of meter has specific software. If you're interested, contact the meter manufacturer. They'll tell you how to get it and what it costs. Insurance plans don't cover software or cables.

- **Language.** Some meter systems can display in English, Spanish, or up to seven other languages.

- **Battery and machine replacement.** Just like flashlights and TV remote controls, meters need batteries. Each model handles batteries differently. A few have permanent batteries, which usually last for a few years. Then you have to replace the meter. For most meters, the batteries are standard electronic-equipment batteries. You buy the replacements and insert them yourself. Depending on how often you test, batteries can last months to years. It's always best to have one on hand before you need it.

- **Your insurance coverage.** Your insurance program or company health plan may want you to use a specific meter. Check this out before you buy and also find out if you're covered for the strips.

- **Your need/desire for other test results.** A few blood glucose meters also test for lipids, ketones, and glycated proteins. These features are usually not needed unless your doctor suggests you need to do these tests at home.

Who Pays?

Most states require that insurance plans cover meters and strips. If your insurance offers meters and strips through a mail-order or prescription benefit program, you'll need to get a prescription to be reimbursed.

If you don't have insurance, you can almost always find a deal on a meter with rebates and special purchase offers. Check with your diabetes educator or pharmacist and keep an eye on ads. Check the *Diabetes Forecast* Shopper's Guide. You'll probably find a bargain, especially in shopping for strips.

Medicare covers glucose meters, test strips, and lancets. The supplier must submit the claim. For more information about Medicare's coverage of diabetes supplies, contact:

The Center for Medicare and Medicaid Services
    (CMS)
7500 Security Blvd.
Baltimore, MD 21244
1-800-MEDICARE (1–800–633–4227) (English
    and Spanish)
TTY/TDD 1–877–486–2048
www.medicare.gov

No Matter Which Meter You Choose . . .

■ **When you buy your meter,** be sure it has been set to the correct date and time. Ask

your pharmacist or diabetes educator to
show you how.

- **Test your machine and strips for accuracy** using a standard control solution.
These solutions have a known concentration of glucose that you compare to your
meter's result. Do this monthly or according to manufacturer's instructions, and also
when you suspect your meter is not working correctly.

- **Take your meter with you** for diabetes
appointments. Take a meter reading within
a few minutes of having blood drawn for
laboratory glucose tests. Compare the
results. If your meter is off by more than
15%, call the manufacturer for possible
replacement.

Finger-Sticking Devices and Lancets

Meters always come with a lancet device
but there are several kinds of lancing devices and
lancets. The devices often have adjustments for
how deep the lancets poke into your finger or they
have separate caps that control depth. Use the shallowest poke possible to draw blood—it hurts less.
If your device comes without an adjustment or it
hurts too much for you, talk to your diabetes educator about finding a device that's right for you.

Some people use lancets without the lancing device to sample their blood. This takes some practice and usually hurts more.

If you have dexterity limitations, look for an automatic lancing device that resets easily with a simple push-pull movement.

Where to Buy

Some pharmacies specialize in diabetes supplies, carrying many brands of meters and other supplies. In addition to medical supplies, you may find books, low-calorie foods, and information on local diabetes events and organizations.

Diabetes supply specialty stores offer another shopping option. To find one, call your local ADA chapter, or check in the phone book under "Medical Supplies" or "Diabetes." If you're lucky enough to have one in the neighborhood, you may be able to one-stop-shop for many non-prescription items. In diabetes shops, you can actually compare models, ask questions, and receive training on complicated tools.

You might choose to use mail-order. Order your strips and other equipment at least two weeks in advance. If you have insurance, starting up with a mail-order house takes some time up-front. They must confirm your insurance coverage before filling your first order.

Testing?

Today I "Interviewed" a new doctor, and was totally shocked. From what I have learned in the education course, carbs and testing are important parts of controlling diabetes. This doctor told me to throw away my monitor and stop testing. He said the only test that counts is the A1C.
—K

DO NOT TAKE THE ADVICE OF THE DOCTOR YOU MENTIONED. . . . Good Luck. —j

Re: Testing?

As far as that doctor is concerned, you should get plenty of exercise when you RUN SCREAMING from his office. In every medical school, there are people who finish at the top of their class, and there are people who hang out with the janitor during study hall. I think you found that guy. The only thing missing there is a chicken's foot. Seriously, the suggestion that you may find a doctor more comfortable with diabetes by asking around at your education classes is right on the money. Whichever way you try, just be sure to trust your instincts when you meet the physicians, and be sure that you work with someone you feel comfortable with. You picked your friends in life, and probably did okay with that, so use that knowledge again. Good luck, and keep us posted. We're a nosy bunch here, but it's all good. —w

Re: Testing?
You guys hit my gut instinct here! As I left his office and drove to work, the further I got, the most I was uncomfortable with his reasoning. Personally it scares me to death knowing that I have diabetes and a doctor does NOT want me to test. I realize that diabetes education is forever changing, however I have lost 4 loved ones in my life due to complications of diabetes, and what stands out is, I don't remember EVER seeing any of them test! Being newly diagnosed and having learned what I did in the education course, I feel it important to test at least 2x per day, more if you feel you need to learn how you react to certain foods, and exercise. I will keep you all updated, and yes I am still looking for

another doctor! I still have the endo appointment September 9th. —K

Re: Newly Diagnosed and Scared.
YOU NEED TO CHECK YOUR BLOOD SUGAR . . . so try to get a monitor as soon as you can. The day I was diagnosed, my doc. loaned me a monitor until I could get to the drugstore and get my own. Good luck . . . —j2

Re: Newly Diagnosed and Scared.
I agree completely. GET A METER. Your insurance should cover it AND the supplies as long as you have a prescription. This means an immediate visit to your doctor's office. If you are going to have to pay yourself, check out STRIP prices first. Then go with the meter that will cost you the least in supplies but does what you need. Final note—I have been talking with others in my Yahoo! group, and we all differ on lancets. My opinion (and I was told this in the diabetes class as well) is that as long as your hands are clean, you DON'T test on anyone else, and the lancet is still sharp

enough—keep on using it! Best wishes.
—sm

Re: Newly Diagnosed and Scared.
Hi j2, hope you are doing well. Taking
blood sugar (bs) readings with a meter
can really work for you. One of the ways
I use my bs readings is to evaluate which
foods cause my bs to rise too high. For
example, if I eat a banana my bs count
goes sky high (my stock should go up
that fast). I then experiment, I eat a half
of a banana and test my bs (not on the
same day). I do this with all my food
intake. In the beginning I kept a log and I
could then compare how each food and
portion affected my bs. After awhile I no
longer needed to keep the log. There is no
one exact diet for all diabetics. Everyone
must find their own list of foods that
work best for them. By the way I am on
ACTOS and it works great. My readings
are right on the money (85 to 105 two
hours after meals). YOU can control diabetes, it takes time and planning. Please
keep in contact and God Bless. —CM

Ok I'm ready to get serious cuz,,,

Hey all, Yes I'm a newbie! Ok, Here goes! I was diagnosed 6 yrs or so ago with type 2 diabetes, I haven't took it serious till as of late, I've been on medication during this time, about a yr ago I changed to glucovance 5/500mgs once in morn once in evening and actos 30mgs, I haven't watched what I eat and been to the doc on regular visits as of late, the last time I seen the doc, I fasted all night and my sugar that morn was 175, so he doubled my medication to 2 in morn 2 in evening of glucovance 5/500mgs, I'm worried now cuz I still haven't adhered to a diet and or eating right, did quit smoking after 25 yrs {2nd week}, I checked my sugar this morn and it was 356! I'm worried cuz the doc said I was headed to insulin dependence! I'm wondering if it's too late now to start doing what I'm supposed to! or is it too late! I know you people aren't doctors but can anybody share an experience with me! —S

Re: Ok I'm ready to get serious cuz,,,

You sound very similar to me. Diagnosed about 6 yrs ago, put on Glucophage but I pretty much ignored diet, exercise and testing. Recently I started taking it very seriously, test 3–4 times daily, eating much better and exercising (treadmill) 30 minutes a day 3x per week. Doc also put me on 4mg Amaryl per day. I am now averaging between 80 and about 160 all the time. NO! It's not too late . . . take control. I feel better and really enjoy using a program called GlucoPilot on my Palm to track my reading . . . my doc likes it too as he can get a very good idea from the graphs where I am and how I'm doing! I found that the exercise was VERY important as it had an immediate effect on my blood sugar readings (drops by 20–50 pts after exercise). It's really cool being able to see the effect of different foods and exercise and the feeling of being in control. —C

4

Oral Medications

When you were diagnosed with diabetes, you may have left your doctor's office with a prescription in hand. The medication addresses one of four possible problems that have been keeping your blood glucose levels too high.

Sulfonylureas

Problem: Your pancreas doesn't produce enough insulin throughout the day.

Drugs called **sulfonylureas** help your pancreas produce more insulin.

Sulfonylureas are the elder statesmen of oral medications. They've been on the market for over 50 years, and for much of that time, they were the only type of oral medication available to treat type 2 diabetes in the United States. Because they've been on the market for years, side effects and drug interactions are well known, and many are available as generics.

The oldest (first-generation) sulfonylureas are seldom used now that better sulfonylureas are available.

Side Effects

A possible side effect of sulfonylureas is **hypoglycemia,** or low blood sugar. If you develop a low while on a sulfonylurea, it could last for hours.

As with some of the other diabetes meds, you may **gain weight** when you go on a sulfonylurea. When your blood glucose levels are high, some glucose, and therefore calories, are lost in your urine. When you get better control of your diabetes, you no longer lose those calories. Or it could be that when you start a new medication, you think, "This new pill will take care of everything—I can eat whatever I want." And your weight creeps up.

A modest weight gain may be offset by the health

Table 4-1. Sulfonylureas

	Generic Name	Brand Names	Available as a generic?	Comments, Cautions
First-generation (Seldom used)	chlorpropamide	Diabinese	yes	Chlorpropamide is the longest-acting sulfonylurea, so it has an increased potential to cause hypoglycemia. It's not recommended for elderly patients and those with kidney disease. It may cause low blood sodium levels, jaundice, and possibly skin rashes.
	tolazamide	Tolinase	yes	Patients with kidney disease may need smaller doses.
	tolbutamide	Orinase	yes	Shortest-acting sulfonylurea. Less potential for hypoglycemia. May be good choice for elderly or those with liver or kidney disease. It's taken two or three times a day, so it's not a good choice if you often forget to take pills.

continued

Table 4-1. Sulfonylureas (*Continued*)

	Generic Name	Brand Names	Available as a generic?	Comments, Cautions
Second-generation (Most used)	glimepiride	Amaryl	no	Probably safe in people with kidney disease, but a patient with kidney disease or who is elderly should be started on lower-than-usual dose.
	glipizide	Glucotrol	yes	Should be taken a half-hour before meals to be most effective.
	glipizide (long-acting)	Glucotrol XL	no	Can be taken with a meal.
	glyburide	DiaBeta, Micronase	yes	Intermediate-acting, but effects may last entire day.
	glyburide (micronized)	Glynase PresTab	yes	More readily absorbed than regular glyburide, therefore the strengths of the tablets are different.

benefits of lower blood glucose levels. And gaining weight isn't inevitable. Talk to your dietitian about meal planning to avoid weight gain.

Metformin

Problem: Your liver releases glucose when it's not needed.

Metformin's main action is to keep your liver from releasing too much glucose. It also makes muscle cells more sensitive to insulin.

Metformin has been on the market in the United States since 1995 and is now available as a generic. Metformin has been used in other countries for over 30 years.

Unlike many other diabetes medications (sulfonylureas, TZDs, and insulin), metformin does not cause weight gain. You may even lose a few pounds when you start using metformin because you may find that you're not as hungry. Another advantage: Your LDL and triglyceride levels may decrease a bit. Metformin does not cause hypoglycemia.

Generic Name	Brand Names	Available as a generic?
metformin	Glucophage	yes
metformin (long-acting)	Glucophage XR	no

Side Effects

Common side effects in the beginning are **nausea, diarrhea,** and **stomach cramping.** These usually last only a few weeks. To minimize these, your doctor will start you on a low dose and slowly work you up to the dose you need to control your blood sugars.

You can reduce these side effects by taking metformin with a meal. If you're troubled by diarrhea when you start metformin, don't eat any dairy products (milk, cheese) for a time.

A rare, serious side effect of metformin is **lactic acidosis.** This can occur in people whose kidneys don't function properly or who have severe heart or respiratory disease. Metformin may not be right for you if you:

- are 80 or older
- have kidney problems
- have severe respiratory problems
- are taking medication for heart failure
- have a history of liver disease
- drink alcohol excessively

If you're scheduled for any medical testing or surgical procedures where you will have to fast or have an iodinated dye injected into your veins, tell the doctor in charge that you take metformin. These tests affect your kidneys and your doctor may want you to stop taking the metformin for a few days.

The Glitazones

Problem: Insulin resistance especially in your muscle and fat cells.

TZDs (full name thiazo-lidinediones, also called glitazones) do many things, but the most important things they do is make muscle and fat cells more sensitive to insulin and preserve the ability of your pancreas to produce insulin.

TZDs are often used in combination with other medications but may be used alone. It typically takes four to six weeks to see an effect on your blood glucose.

Like many medications, TZDs are cleared by your liver. Therefore, you need a blood test for liver function done before starting rosiglitazone or pioglitazone and every two months for the first year. Your doctor may order liver tests periodically after that.

Generic Name	Brand Names	Available as a generic?
pioglitazone	Actos	no
rosiglitazone	Avandia	no

Side Effects

As with other diabetes medications, **weight gain** is possible. A typical gain is 5 to 10 pounds; some people gain more.

If you notice a rapid weight gain, the added weight could be from **fluid retention.** Other signs of fluid retention are swelling of the feet or ankles (you might notice that your socks or shoes are leaving imprints in your skin) and shortness of breath. This is more common if you also use insulin.

When the weight gained with TZDs is fat, it's usually not the abdominal fat that's associated with insulin resistance and other health problems. But that's little comfort when you're looking at your bathroom scale.

It would be prudent to weigh yourself weekly for the first six months you're on a TZD, especially months two and three, when the TZD is getting up to its full effect. If you go over the typical weight gain or you notice any signs of fluid retention, tell your doctor right away. Excess fluid may put a strain on your heart, if you're susceptible. You may be taken off the TZD and perhaps given a medication to get rid of the excess fluid. Because of the risk of fluid retention, TZDs are not recommended for people with heart failure.

If the weight is not fluid, but fat, discuss with your health care team whether the good (improved blood glucose control) outweighs the bad.

Women: If you aren't ovulating and haven't gone through menopause, a TZD may cause you to ovulate again, and you could get pregnant. Also, oral contraceptives may be less effective if you take pioglitazone. Talk to your doctor about effective birth control methods or using a different TZD.

Problem: Your pancreas doesn't respond quickly after a meal.

You know the fable of the tortoise and the hare. Your pancreas is like the tortoise. It creeps along, producing a low level of insulin. Then along comes the hare: a meal. The starches and sugars are quickly broken down into glucose, and your blood glucose level goes up. And your pancreas? Still creeping along, falling further and further behind. So one to two hours after the meal, your blood sugar is too high. Eventually your pancreas catches up. But for good health, you want a more closely matched race from the start.

You need to get your pancreas to sprint when it needs to, or you need to slow down the glucose surge. Or both.

A **glitinide** will stimulate your pancreas to produce more insulin when it senses the rise in glucose from a meal. You take a glitinide right before each meal or large snack.

Side Effects

These medications can make your blood glucose drop too low if you take them without eating. Don't take a glitinide if you're skipping a meal.

Generic Name	Brand Names	Available as a generic?
nateglinide	Starlix	no
repaglinide	Prandin	no

Alpha-glucosidase inhibitors take the opposite approach to solving the same problem. These drugs slow down the glucose by affecting the digestive process.

About 20 minutes after you eat, the food starts to enter your small intestine. There, enzymes break down the starches and sugars. Starch (for example potato, bread, or pasta) breaks down into many molecules of glucose. This occurs in the first third of the small intestine, and from there, the glucose moves quickly into the bloodstream.

What would happen if just a little starch was broken down in the first third of your intestine, while some starch traveled a little further downstream before being broken down? Glucose absorption would take place over a longer period of time. Instead of a Mount Everest spike in blood glucose, you'd get a longer, flatter hill. Your pancreas would be able to keep up with this more gradual demand.

That's what alpha-glucosidase inhibitors

(AGIs) do. When you take an AGI with the first bite of your meal, the medication ends up in the upper third of your small intestine at the same time your food does. There, the drug inhibits the enzymes that break down starch into glucose. Some starch is broken down, but much of it travels further through the intestine before being broken down.

Generic Name	Brand Names	Available as a generic?
acarbose	Precose	no
miglitol	Glyset	no

Sugars

So far, we've talked about starch. AGIs slow down the breakdown of all starches. Their effect on sugar depends on the type of sugar.

There are two types of sugars. Single sugars (monosaccharides) and double sugars (disaccharides).

Single sugars don't need to be broken down in the intestine. They're already small enough to be absorbed. Therefore, foods that contain mostly single sugars won't be affected by AGIs.

▪ **Glucose** is a single sugar. The gels and tabs designed for the treatment of insulin reactions contain glucose. Corn syrup is mostly glucose.

■ **Fructose** is a single sugar. Fruits contain

Alpha-glucosidase inhibitors **slow the digestion** of the following carbohydrates. When you take an alpha-glucosidase inhibitor with the first bite of these foods, your blood glucose levels won't go up as quickly.

Breads

Crackers

Cereals

Grains: rice, bulgur, millet

Pasta

Beans

Potatoes

Table sugar, brown sugar, powdered sugar

Maple syrup, molasses

Alpha-glucosidase inhibitors have **little or no effect** on the digestion of the following carbohydrates. Your blood glucose levels will go up just as quickly after eating these foods whether you take an alpha-glucosidase inhibitor or not.

Glucose: gels, tablets

Milk: skim, 1%, 2%, whole

Plain yogurt, sugar-free yogurt

Corn syrup

Honey

Fruits

fructose, as well as sucrose and glucose.

- **Sucrose** (table sugar) is a double sugar. It's a glucose attached to a fructose. Sucrose does need to be split. So AGIs do slow the breakdown of sucrose.
- **Lactose,** the sugar found in milk, is a double sugar, but it needs a different enzyme—lactase—to break it down. AGIs don't inhibit lactase, so they don't slow the breakdown of lactose.

Side Effects

A very common side effect of AGIs is intestinal gas, including bloating and flatulence. This happens when undigested carbohydrate ends up in the large intestine, where bacteria feed on it and produce gas. Ask your doctor about starting with a low dose and increasing gradually. For example, you might start with a low dose with the first bite of one meal a day and work up to taking the AGI with each meal.

Unlike many other diabetes meds, AGIs do not cause weight gain.

AGIs don't cause hypoglycemia when used alone. If you also take a sulfonylurea, meglitinide, or insulin, hypoglycemia can occur. If it does, use pure glucose (tablets, gel) to treat the low. Because AGIs interfere with the digestion of many other carbohydrate, they won't work as fast to treat a low blood sugar.

Who Shouldn't Take: Because these medications work directly in the intestines, people with inflammatory bowel disease, other intestinal diseases, or obstructions should not take these medications.

Which Drug?

How does your doctor know which of the four problems is your biggest problem, and therefore which medication to prescribe?

Diabetes care, like much of medicine, is part science, part art. When deciding which medication to prescribe, your doctor will consider:

- Your blood glucose levels. There are no hard and fast rules, but if your blood sugars are very high your doctor may prescribe a combination of diabetes medications including insulin to bring them down more quickly. Other things your doctor will consider are:
- Your other lab results (cholesterol levels, etc.).
- Your age.
- Your weight.
- Your other medical conditions, such as kidney, liver, or heart problems.
- Whether you're pregnant or planning to get

pregnant. Oral agents are not recommended during pregnancy. You'll need to use insulin.

▦ Whether you have diabetes complications.

▦ Other medications you're taking, because some may interact with some diabetes drugs. Make a list or bring in (to your doctor and your pharmacist):

● Over-the-counter medications.

● Herbal and other alternative remedies.

● Vitamins and supplements.

● A record of how much alcohol you drink and when you drink it.

● At least a mental record of your recreational drug use.

Talk openly with your doctor, so he or she will also be able to take into account:

▦ Whether you can afford a newer drug that is not available as a less expensive generic.

▦ Whether you often forget to take pills. If so, a pill that needs to be taken three times a day may not be the best choice.

Starting

For many of the drugs, your doctor will start you with a low dose of the drug and build up from there. You'll be asked to check your blood glucose levels to see how well the drug is working for you.

Different diabetes medications exert their effects at different times. Be sure to ask your doctor or pharmacist when the best time is to check blood sugars and how often for the medication(s) you take. Once you get to a dose that's working for you, you may be able to check your blood sugars less often.

If a drug works for you, you can expect to see a drop in your A1C. The ADA recommends an A1C of less than 7%. If your A1C is more than 7% talk to your health care providers about what can be done to get to goal.

Combination Therapy

Type 2 diabetes is a progressive disease. As you get older, your beta cells make less and less insulin. You might also gain a few pounds and be less active, which makes your insulin resistance worse. You'll need additional medications to reach your blood glucose goals. In the UKPDS, three years after diagnosis, about half the patients needed more than one medication to reach their blood glucose goals. Nine years after diagnosis, 75% needed more than one medication to reach their goals.

As you've seen, there are several causes of high blood sugars. For your second medication, your doctor will choose an oral agent that treats a different problem than the first drug is treating. Or you may start to use insulin rather than add a second or third oral agent.

Combination therapy is so common that some drug companies now market combination pills. One advantage is that you take only one pill at a time, and you pay only one co-pay for the prescription. Disadvantages are your doctor may not be able to up the dose of one of the medications without upping the dose of the other. And no generic (less expensive) versions of combo pills are on the market yet. The combo pills available are:

Brand Name	Generic Ingredients
Avandamet	metformin + rosiglitazone (a TZD)
Glucovance	metformin + glyburide (a sulfonylurea)
Metaglip	metformin + glipizide (a sulfonylurea)

To sum up the treatments that lower your blood sugar, look at Table 4-2. You may want to put more energy each day into the non-drug treatments of physical activity, meal planning, and weight loss. These improve your health in all areas and save you money and side effects that may come with drug treatments.

Focus On: What About Diet and Exercise Alone?

In years past, "diet-and-exercise" was touted as the first-line treatment for type 2 diabetes. According to this old plan, only when diet and exercise "failed"

Table 4-2. Actions of Diabetes Treatments

	Increase insulin secretion	Increase insulin sensitivity (reduce insulin resistance) in muscle/fat cells	Reduce glucose spikes from a meal	Reduce glucose output from liver
Oral Medications				
Sulfonylureas	***			
Metformin		*		***
TZDs		***	*	*
Glitinides	***			
Alpha-glucosidase inhibitors			***	
Non-drug Treatments				
Physical activity		***		
Meal planning			***	
Weight loss		***		***

were oral agents added to the treatment plan.

First, diet and exercise don't "fail." Being physically active and eating a healthy diet with special attention to the carbohydrate will help you reach your blood glucose, blood pressure, and cholesterol goals throughout your life.

These will *help* you reach your goals—but diet and exercise probably can't do the whole job for you. Remember that at diagnosis, the typical person has had diabetes for eight to ten years. That far into the disease process, most people need medication—either an oral agent or insulin—to get their blood glucose levels down to near the non-diabetic range.

We know this from the United Kingdom Prospective Diabetes Study (UKPDS). Early on in the study, the researchers looked at the response to diet therapy of 3,044 people newly diagnosed with type 2 diabetes. The average age of these patients was 52 years, average body weight was 30% above ideal, average fasting blood glucose was 218 mg/dl. They received intensive nutrition education from dietitians for three months.

The goal set in the study was a fasting blood glucose of 108 mg/dl—in other words, within the nondiabetic range, which the study would go on to prove greatly reduces the risk of some diabetes complications.

Only 16% of the patients achieved this goal after three months of diet therapy. Of those with a starting fasting glucose of less than 144 mg/dl, 50% reached the goal. Of those with starting fasting glucose levels of 288 mg/dl to 396 mg/dl, only 10% reached the goal of 108 mg/dl with diet therapy alone. Subjects who started out with a fasting plasma glucose of 180 mg/dl to 216 mg/dl needed to lose about 40 pounds, on average, to reach the fasting blood glucose goal of less than 108 mg/dl.

Three years after diagnosis, only 8% were still reaching their goals with diet therapy alone, at six years it was 5%, and at nine years, 4%.

Should people newly found to have diabetes always rely on nutritional therapy alone for a long and often unhappy time before considering the addition of drug therapy? . . . Lifestyle management begins now and continues lifelong, but it rarely does the job alone.

−Matthew C. Riddle, MD
Diabetes Spectrum 13: 194−196, 2000

Will It Work For You?

Could you be one of the minority who can, at least for a few years, get near-normal blood glucose levels without medication? Consider two scenarios:

Let's say you had a physical a couple of years ago, and your fasting blood glucose was normal. Shortly after that, your company started to "right size." You sweated through six months of lay-offs. Your job was spared, but then you were doing the work of a person and a half. You dealt with the stress by eating junk food, and you gained weight. You were working long hours, so you didn't have time to do your usual biking and golfing. Then your father, who lives in another state, started to show signs of Alzheimer's.

Stress makes the liver release glucose. Weight gain and inactivity increase insulin resistance. You've just had another fasting glucose test, and it's 150 mg/dl.

Your fasting blood glucose is high enough for diabetes to be diagnosed, but it's not sky high, so you're still making a fair amount of insulin. You know you caught your diabetes early. And your lifestyle is about to take a turn for the better. You found a reliable care-taker for your father, and you just switched to a less stressful job. You feel sure you can drop the extra pounds you gained, and now you have the time to exercise.

You might do well with meal planning and exercise alone.

Since meal planning will be your main treatment, see a registered dietitian so you can take full advantage of what meal planning can do for you.

In the UKPDS, if diet alone was going to do the trick, it worked within six weeks to three months. If your blood glucose levels are still above your goals after that time, see your doctor.

DIET ALONE DIDN'T CUT IT

James Thomas was diagnosed with type 2 diabetes when he was 29. At first, he refused to believe his doctor. "I was like, He doesn't know what he's talking about," says Thomas.

"The doctor said we would try to control it through my diet. He told me he was sending me to a dietitian. But I was being hard-headed and didn't see the dietitian."

Thomas found himself getting up in the middle of the night to go to the bathroom, and he was tired all the time. "As time went on, I could see what the doctor was talking about. I started trying to follow the doctor's directions."

Thomas started taking an oral agent, eating less, and exercising regularly. He lost 40 pounds.

"It's better," he says. "I can see the difference. I don't run to the bathroom all through the night and feel tired during the day. Physically, I feel a lot better, a lot stronger."

Scenario 2: You've just been diagnosed with diabetes, with a fasting blood glucose of over 300 mg/dl. The diagnosis wasn't a surprise. Looking back, you can see that for a number of years you've been more and more tired, and you've been getting up in the middle of the night to use the bathroom.

Your whole life you've battled the bulge with no lasting success. You've always been fairly inactive. And right now, you feel defeated.

You're probably not a good candidate for diet therapy alone. If you try it and your blood sugars don't come down, you've gone another one or three or six months feeling sicker than you need to.

Imagine taking a different tack: You get on the right medication, and after two increases, it's at the right dose. You feel better within weeks. Your meter shows that your blood glucose levels are down.

Meanwhile, you see a dietitian. Meal planning helps your blood sugars come down even more. You start to have more energy. You begin a moderate walking program. You feel even better. And you realize: This is the way to go.

DID IT WITH DIET

A typical day for Deborah Jones started with a Pepsi. Reese's peanut butter cups for a mid-morning snack. Junk food the rest of the day washed down with three or four cans of Pepsi. Two liters of Pepsi at night. Jones estimates that 80% of her calories came from Pepsi and candy.

"I did not sit down and eat a regular meal," she says. "I ate junk all day long. Even when I wasn't eating junk, I would still be eating meat or something else high fat."

When she was diagnosed with high blood pressure, her doctor advised her to change her diet and start an exercise program, but Jones didn't.

A few years later, a friend of Jones' died of a heart attack. That scared Jones into seeing a dietitian for help in losing weight. The dietitian advised Jones to get tested for diabetes. Jones did, and was found to have a glucose level of 300 mg/dl. "It was a slap in the face," says Jones.

She told her doctor she would change her lifestyle this time. "He gave me two weeks to do it with dieting, and if not, he'd put me on medication. 'I don't think you're going to do it,' is what he said."

Jones quit Pepsi that day and, armed with the exchange lists her dietitian and doctor had given her, went to the grocery store to buy non-junk food. She started exercising on a stationary bike.

Two weeks later, she went back to her doctor. Her blood glucose level was 150 mg/dl. Her doctor told her to keep doing what she was doing.

Jones worked closely with her dietitian and went to diabetes education classes. She rode her bike 30 minutes a day, often seeing her blood glucose drop 30 mg/dl after biking. She lost 40 pounds in five months. Her blood pressure came down and her blood glucose levels stayed down.

"The last time I went to see my doctor, he told me he was proud of me."

A long week

I was told by my Doc on June 11th that my blood sugar was high and although I did not have "many" type 2 symptoms I was probably diabetic. "Cut out the sugars, eat less carbs and get more exercise. Go see the people at the diabetes clinic." It did not sound too serious (BG was 260 at fasting but that number really meant nothing to me). So, a month later I get to the clinic. They say "we're going to do a blood test for glucose" I scored a 230. Nurse says "you really should be on meds." Now I'm scared. Had no idea carbs were important (thought it was sugar). Thank God for the diabetes clinic education program. Anyway ... following the Dietitians food plan to a T. Tonight I had a med. baked potato (3 carb units) and I had a 365 reading 2 hours later. I've had 275–295 eating 3 carb units of other foods. It's been 6 days since I started counting carbs. Is this too soon to expect changes (results) in lowering blood sugar? Does a spike upward of 100 over other levels indicate a serious problem or is this normal for someone newly diagnosed? Sorry for the lengthy post but I'm concerned (scared). I've got a great support network but not a lot who know about diabetes Thanks. —L

Re: A long week

I know everyone is different, but your numbers sound too high to not be on meds. Talk to your doctor, and don't be afraid to get a new doctor if he does not treat this seriously. Good Luck —hj

Re: A long week

You MUST go back to your doctor VERY soon. Most people see some sort of result after a week, although it will take a LONG time to get the average down. Are you exercising at all? Even ten minutes extra a day will help—even gentle walking to start with if you don't have a high activity level at the minute. Also, your doctor needs to know what sort of figures you are getting, and at what times. It may be that the figures are higher than he(?) had thought. Myself, it really does sound as though you need medication to get the levels down NOW, and then use diet and exercise to reduce the meds eventually. Have you had the blood work for the hemoglobin test? This gives a three-month picture of the AVERAGE glucose, and is almost better than the fasting figure to let you know where you are. Use the library, be more involved with your doctor and keep working with the diet people. Everyone is different, but this CAN be beaten. I wish you well. —sm

Re: A long week
I agree that maybe you should speak with your doctor about taking some meds for at least a while, until you can regularly get blood sugar in normal range with new way of eating and exercising. My blood sugar was 350 when I was diagnosed 5 years ago—also with no clue what that figure meant. Luckily, my doctor did, however, and put me on meds, which along with eating better helped get my bs within normal range in about a week. I immediately started walking every day after meals and snacks (just a few minutes, because that was all I was able to do at that time, being 40 pounds overweight and not in the walking habit), but within 2 months I was able to keep blood sugar in control without any meds. About that time

I also saw a Registered Dietitian who helped me learn how to read labels and count carbs and combine foods for well-balanced meals and snacks—high fiber, low fat, low calorie. She gave me some great ideas. I gradually cut back on the food portion sizes as I increased my exercise. I think the thing is that you have to balance what you eat with how active you are, and how much you get your metabolism revved-up, whether with exercise or meds, or a combination thereof, and keep up with changes in your body over a period of time, such as if you lose a certain amount of weight, you would not need to eat as much, but you'd need to step up the exercise in order to continue to burn the same amount of calories and blood sugar as when you weighed more. Well, that's been my overall plan, and as far as potatoes go, I cut them in half, thirds, or quarters, depending on their size, and combine them with protein, fiber, and some "good" fat to make a well-balanced healthy meal followed by exercise. So, you got a 365 two hours after eating a medium potato, but what was your bs before dinner, and how did you get it down afterwards? It's a good idea to make sure that your pre-meal bs is within normal range, and then after dinner your exercise and/or meds should take care of your post-meal bs levels. — pw

Re: A long week
Thank you for your replies. I was at 205 before dinner and 365 two hours later. I love baked potatoes and figured 7 ounces to 3 carb units. No other carbs at dinner or food between checks. This morning I'm at 203 before breakfast and had 2 carb units at that meal. Had a 4-hour presentation (on my feet and moving around) and before lunch I'm at 233. I'm frustrated but will take your advice and call the doc about meds. Thanks again. —L

5

Meal Planning

Meal planning will help you reach your blood glucose, blood pressure, and cholesterol goals. It is a vital part of the treatment plan for your diabetes and metabolic syndrome.

This chapter will give you an introduction to a few meal planning tools for blood glucose control. (Meal planning for blood pressure and cholesterol control are covered in their chapters.) As you read, you might think, "This is kind of complicated." It is. When you think about it, your medication plan is a cinch. Your doctor decides which drug and what dose you need. You take your pills at the same time each day without much thought.

In contrast, you decide several times a day what and how much to eat, and those decisions affect your blood glucose levels. And your strategies change through the years as your medication plan and goals change.

This chapter can't cover all the possibilities. You really need a meal plan designed just for you, your goals, and your likes and dislikes. For this, see a registered dietitian who has experience in diabetes. Dietitians are not the diet police. A good dietitian listens to your goals, considers your other health issues, and gives you the tools and support you need to succeed. Studies show that working with a registered dietitian, called medical nutrition therapy, lowers A1C by 1% to 2%—the same improvement you get with one oral agent.

Meal planning can help you with two of the problems that keep your blood sugars too high.

Problem: Your pancreas doesn't respond quickly after a meal.
One Solution: Carbohydrate counting.

Problem: You're insulin resistant.
One Solution: Weight loss. (Just a little does a lot.)

Carbohydrate Counting

You get calories from fat, protein, and carbohydrate.

Carbohydrate is the general term for starches and sugar. Starch is long chains of glucose molecules. Sucrose (table sugar) is a short chain of just two molecules, one of which is glucose.

Proteins are made up of long chains of amino acids. Most fat in the diet is made up of molecules called triglycerides.

When you eat, carbohydrate is quickly broken down into glucose. Little of the fat and protein you eat turns up as glucose. Therefore, meal planning for diabetes focuses on carbohydrate.

When the glucose from the carbohydrate in a meal hits your bloodstream, you need a burst of insulin to move that glucose into your cells. But because you have diabetes, your pancreas doesn't respond quickly. Your blood glucose stays too high until your pancreas can catch up.

You can make things easier for your pancreas by not eating too much carbohydrate in a single sitting. Carbohydrate counting helps you with this.

Where's the Carb?

The first step in carbohydrate counting is finding out which foods have a lot of carb and which have little or none.

You may be familiar with the Food Guide

Diabetes Food Pyramid

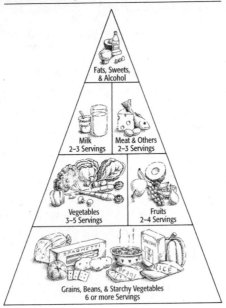

Pyramid. It's on many food packages. (Check your bread.)

The American Diabetes Association and The American Dietetic Association adapted the Food Guide Pyramid for people with diabetes. A few foods were shifted into different sections based on how they affect blood glucose levels.

Starchy vegetables—potatoes, corn, peas—were moved to the bottom layer, with the grains. A cup of peas or other starchy vegetable will raise your blood glucose more than, say, a cup of spinach.

Beans have protein, but they also have carbohydrate, unlike other protein foods such as fish and eggs. So beans were moved to the section with grains as well.

From the bottom up, foods with notable amounts of carbohydrate are:

▨ Grains, Beans, and Starchy Vegetables
▨ Fruits
▨ Milk Products
▨ Sweets

Are the carbohydrates different in these different sections? Yes and no.

No, they're not different. In terms of the effect these carbohydrate foods have on your blood glucose levels, no, they are not different from each other. Two hours after a meal, a serving (1/2 cup) of mashed potatoes will have raised your blood glucose about as much as a serving (1/8 pie) of custard pie. You read that right: Despite bad press, sugar really isn't off-limits to people with diabetes.

However . . .

Yes, they're different. In terms of overall health, some sections are better than others. Whole grains, beans, and starchy vegetables provide vitamins, minerals, and fiber. Notice that their section is the biggest, meaning a healthy diet has more servings from this section than from the other sections.

Fruit also provides vitamins, minerals, and fiber, and no cholesterol nor (with very few exceptions) saturated fat.

Milk products contain vitamins and minerals. Fat-free dairy products, or milk substitutes such as soy milk, are healthy. But other dairy foods (whole or 2% milk, cheese, sour cream) have saturated fat, which is bad for your heart.

Sweets, as your mother may have told you, are empty calories—calories with little if any vitamins, minerals, or fiber. Sweets are often mixed with fat (think of chocolate and pastries), so they often have a lot of empty calories. They're in the smallest section of the pyramid; a healthy diet has few servings of sweets. That's true whether you have diabetes or not.

Using Carb Counting

Using the Diabetes Food Pyramid, which breakfast has more carbohydrate?

1: soft-boiled egg on one slice of plain toast, black coffee
2: pancakes, syrup, orange juice

Breakfast #2 has more carb. Pancakes are from the Grain section, syrup is from the Sweets section, orange juice is from Fruit. In breakfast #2, only the toast has carb.

Will your blood glucose level be higher after breakfast #2? Find out for yourself. Check your blood glucose level before a meal and write down the result. Eat one of your favorite meals that you now know has a lot of carb. Check your blood glucose level one to two hours after you start eating the meal. How much did your blood sugar go up?

The next day at the same time, eat a low-carb meal, checking your blood glucose before and after. Or eat the same meal but substitute low- or no-carb foods for some of the high-carb foods. (If you're using insulin or taking a sulfonylurea or a meglitinide, check with your doctor, dietitian, or diabetes educator before doing this experiment.)

"I ate four instead of a half dozen."

I stopped eating sugar, period. I cut down on eating a loaf of bread a day. I still don't do all the things my wife wants me to. I'm not supposed to eat a lot of rolls, but I have a soft spot in my heart for rolls. So last time we went out, I ate four instead of a half dozen. I was still hungry, so I ate some rabbit food—a salad.

— James Thomas

For example, say you normally eat a big plate of spaghetti and four slices of garlic bread, all washed down with regular soda. The next day, try a little less spaghetti, a salad instead of three slices of garlic bread, and a no-calorie (and, therefore, no-carb) drink, such as diet soda, water, or iced tea with artificial sweetener.

How Much Carb?

Did you find that the high-carb meal put your blood sugars way above your goal, while the lower-carb meal kept your blood sugars closer to your goal? (You're shooting for under 180 mg/dl one to two hours after a meal.) How do you apply these results to other meals? How much carb is too much for you at one sitting?

You need to know how much carb different

Spaghetti

Nutrition Facts

Serving Size 2 oz dry

Servings Per Container 4

Amount Per Serving

Calories 210   Calories from Fat 10

Total Fat 1g

Saturated Fat 0g

Cholesterol 0mg

Sodium 280mg

Total Carbohydrate 41g

Dietary Fiber 2g

Sugars 2g

Protein 7g

Ready-to-Heat Garlic Bread

Nutrition Facts
Serving Size 1/5 loaf (57g)
Servings Per Container 5
Amount Per Serving
Calories 200 Calories from Fat 80
Total Fat 9g
Saturated Fat 1.5g
Cholesterol 0mg
Sodium 320mg
Total Carbohydrate 25g
Dietary Fiber 1g
Sugars 1g
Protein 4g

foods contain. An easy way is to look at the
Nutrition Facts on packaged foods. Look at
Serving Size and Total Carbohydrate. (Don't
worry about the Sugars line. Those grams are
already counted in Total Carbohydrate.)
Your high-carb meal is:

	Carb
Spaghetti, 2 cups cooked (4 oz dry),	82g
Garlic bread, 2 servings	50g
Cola, 2 cans	78g
Total	**210g**

You've found that your high-carb meal is too

much for your body to handle, and now you've figured out how many grams of carbohydrate that is. (At 210g, it's more carbohydrate than many people need in an entire day.)

Next, check your blood sugars before and after other favorite meals. Figure out how much carb those meals have. You'll soon have a good idea how much carb you can eat at different meals and still stay within your goals. The amount of carbohydrate your body can handle at one time is sometimes called your "carbohydrate tolerance." Your carbohydrate tolerance may be different at different times of the day, because you are more insulin resistant at certain times of the day.

When you see a dietitian for the first time, you may be asked to keep a record of everything you eat for several days. Your dietitian can look at your food records and your blood glucose log to estimate your glucose tolerance.

Your dietitian may give you a range of carbohydrate to eat at each meal and snack. The recommendations will be based on your blood glucose records; your age, body weight, and activity level; whether you're trying to lose weight; your other medical conditions; and whether you need to eat three square meals or have smaller meals plus snacks. To give you an idea:

	Grams of carb per day (approx.)
Want to lose weight	180
Older women	180
Women	195
Larger women, older men	210
Children, teen girls, active women, most men	240
Teen boys, active men	300

Exchange Lists for Meal Planning

Another way to keep carbohydrate moderate and consistent throughout the day, plus balance other nutrients, is to use an exchange-based meal plan.

In *Exchange Lists for Meal Planning,* by the American Diabetes Association and The American Dietetic Association, foods are split into three large groups: Meat and meat substitutes; Fat; and Carbohydrate, which has these subgroups:

Starch (breads, crackers, cereals, starchy vegetables, pasta)
Fruit (fresh, canned, juice)
Milk
Other carbohydrates (sugars, sweets, desserts)
Vegetables

The exchange lists are lists of foods and their serving sizes. Each exchange has about the same amount of carbohydrate, fat, and protein as every other food on that list. Any food on a list can be exchanged for any other food on the same list.

One starch exchange contains about 15g carbohydrate, 3g protein, 0–1g fat, and 80 calories. The starch list is long; here are just a few examples:

- 1 slice bread
- 1/2 cup grits or unsweetened oatmeal
- 1/3 cup mashed potato

One fruit exchange contains about 15g carbohydrate and 60 calories. Here are examples:

- 1/2 cup apple cider
- 8 dried apricot halves
- 3/4 cup canned mandarin oranges
- 2 tablespoons raisins

One milk exchange contains about 12g carbohydrate and 8g protein. Fat grams and calories vary. Here are examples from the skim milk list, which has 0–3g fat and 90 calories:

- 1 cup skim milk
- 1 cup low-fat fruit-flavored yogurt sweetened with artificial sweetener

A dietitian can work up an exchange meal plan for you. Your meal plan might call for:

Breakfast: 2 Starch, 1 Fruit, and 1 Milk
Lunch: 2 Starch, 2 Vegetable, 2 Fruit, 2 Meat
Supper: 3 Starch, 2 Vegetable, 1 Fruit, 1 Milk, 1 Meat

One morning you might choose oatmeal with raisins, and yogurt. Another morning you might choose cold cereal with fruit and milk. As long as you stick to the general template of 2 Starch, 1 Fruit, and 1 Milk, you'll get about the same amount of carbohydrate at each breakfast. That's good for blood glucose control. When you follow your exchange plan throughout the day, you get a balanced diet with foods from different food groups. That's good for overall health.

Weight Loss

Most people with type 2 diabetes and the metabolic syndrome are overweight. Losing a little weight will improve your health.

You do *not* have to get down to your "ideal" weight to see an improvement in your health. Losing 10 to 20 pounds can make a big difference in your blood sugars, blood pressure, and cholesterol levels. Aim for losing 1/2 to 1 pound per week, or 10 pounds in 3 to 6 months. You'll likely see an improvement after you lose just 5 pounds. Just cutting calories, *before you see any weight loss,* will bring blood glucose levels down.

How to do it? There's no one, great "diet" that will work for everyone. Your dietitian can help you choose a method that will work for you. In the meantime, we can suggest a few ways to cut calories.

Consciousness Raising

(We don't admit to any personal knowledge of the situations described.)

Liquid Candy

If you ate two candy bars every day in addition to your usual meals—60 candy bars a month—would you expect to gain weight?

Let's say you stop on your way to work and pick up a coffee drink with an Italian name, at lunch you get lemonade and accept the free refill, and that night you have two beers. Add up the calories from your drinks, and you'll find it's more calories than you'd get from two candy bars. (Your favorite coffee drink alone might be more than two candy bars. Check out the company's Web site and click on Nutrition Information.)

We often don't think of beverages as food that we have to count. Mentally, we consider the coffee drink a needed pick-me-up, lemonade a thirst quencher (aren't we always being told to stay well hydrated?), and beer goes in the R&R column.

We do the same to our children. When they say, "I'm thirsty," instead of saying, "Drink some water," we hand out fruit-flavored drinks or sodas. That's 100 calories from added sugars.

» Consciousness Raiser

Count the calories and carb of everything you drink for one day. Pay special attention to serving size. Bottles of juice from snack bars are often two servings per bottle. Calories listed are for one serving. Drink the whole bottle and you're getting nearly a candy bar's worth of calories.

Remember to count alcohol. The calories add up more quickly than you might think. A regular beer is about 150 calories; 4 oz. of wine is about 85; a shot of hard liquor, about 100 calories.

Start calling soda and other sugary drinks "liquid candy"—out loud. It gives you pause when you say to your child or grandchild, "Here honey, have a cup of liquid candy."

Drink	Amount	Calories	Carb
Total			

Cutting down on caloric beverages is an easy way to cut calories.

- Drink water or unsweetened tea
- For juice, use a small (4-oz) glass.
- Cut juices and fruit-flavored drinks with club soda or extra water.
- Beware of mocha-latte-frappé drinks. Ask for the Nutrition Facts (calories, carb, saturated fat) of your favorites.

Picky Eater

You made a casserole for dinner. You ate your fill. An hour later, you're putting away the leftovers. You uncover the casserole just to check on it. You eat a nibble. Mmmm, that's good—and just the right temperature. Another nibble. No one's looking, so you're able to dig out the best parts. That was savory, so now you have a taste for something sweet. A nibble of that night's dessert is just right.

You've just eaten another half a meal—and you weren't even hungry. But it didn't seem like a meal, did it? You ate standing up, you didn't dish out a serving—it seemed like just . . . a taste. But it was calories and carbohydrate you didn't need.

» Consciousness Raiser

Make it a personal rule not to eat after the sit-down dinner hour, or after a certain hour, such as 8 p.m. Put leftovers away right after dinner. Put them in the back and pile less appealing foods in front. (If your medication plan requires snacking, portion out the snack ahead of time.)

Always sit down to eat, even for the smallest snack. Heck, make a production of it: Put out a napkin and tableware even if you're just eating two cookies.

And don't do anything else when you eat— don't watch T.V., don't read, don't jot down menus for the next week. Calories have a way of slipping in unnoticed when you're distracted.

Portion Control

You love the Nutrition Facts. You read them all
the time. And according to the calorie counts you
see, you're eating only enough to sustain a hiber-
nating mole.

» Consciousness Raiser

Measure everything you eat for a few days. Use
measuring cups and spoons, and a food scale.
Check the serving size on the Nutrition Facts.
Have you been eating more than you realized?

For a fun activity (well, a sobering activity) check
out the portion sizes you usually eat at:
www.nhlbisupport.com/chd1/visualreality/
visualreality.htm

Identify Your Unconscious Eating

We all have our own unconscious eating habits.
To identify your habits, keep a food diary for at
least three days. Record *everything* you eat and
drink, and how much (measure, don't guess).

Each week, pick a source of unconscious
calories to eliminate. Focus on just one. For
example, for one week, eat nothing from your

spouse's plate (either invited or uninvited). When the week is over, that source of calories will no longer be unconscious. Whenever you lift your fork toward your spouse's plate, you'll remember that you're about to add calories and carb to your meal. Then you can make a choice whether to swoop down and grab a bite.

The next week, don't finish what your child doesn't eat. Keep a log of what you don't eat (half order of French fries, 1/2 cup of mac-n-cheese, two chicken nuggets). After the week is over, add up what you didn't eat. You might decide to stop cleaning your child's plate, or, if you hate to see food wasted, you might choose to serve yourself less food, knowing you'll make up for it by eating your child's leftovers.

(Eating from your spouse's or child's plate or straight from the serving dish are all versions of "It was never on my plate so it doesn't count.")

Eat Only When You're Hungry

(Easier said than done.)

When you were young and had a bad day at school, did your mother comfort you with cookies? When you brought home a good report card, were you rewarded with a trip to the ice cream store?

You learned to eat for reasons other than

hunger. You might have the same habits now as an adult.

Eating to Be Sociable

You eat dinner out with friends. Then someone says, "Let's stop for ice cream!" Even though you are absolutely not hungry, you order a cone. Even if you do resist for a time, your friends' cries of, "You have to! You'll make us feel guilty!" wear down your resolve. Other times you'll hear "Oh, you have to try some of this." Or "Is that all you're having? Don't you like my cooking?"

It's hard to resist peer pressure. Joseph Jones, who has type 2 diabetes, has some advice: "If someone insists on your having a drink, let him pour it. Then waste it. It's not your money—don't worry about it. If they insist that you eat, you can let them put the food on the plate and don't eat it. It's up to you whether you take the last step. We all live with choices. You have to make the choices that are best for you."

Eating When You're Tired

It's three in the afternoon. You're dragging. You can't concentrate. You're just plain tired. So you . . . take a nap? Of course not! This is America! Naps are for the indulgent and lazy! But your body is crying out for something so . . . you eat.

The solution: Buck society and nap. With practice, you'll fall asleep quickly and wake up after just a short nap.

If your boss frowns on naps, recognize that you aren't hungry and try to do something besides eating to get your energy up, such as taking a short walk.

Find Out Your Reasons

When you do your food diary, add a column for "Why I ate this." If you're not keeping a diary, for a week ask yourself "Why" every time you're about to eat. The reasons might be:

I was:

■ hungry (The best reason to eat.)
■ angry
■ bored
■ tired
■ lonely
■ stressed
■ nervous

I ate:

■ to celebrate
■ to avoid something I didn't want to do
■ to reward myself (for finally doing the task I was eating to avoid doing)
■ because the person who cooked the food

would be hurt or insulted if I didn't eat it
■ because the food was there
■ because it tasted good

■ I was going on errands and didn't want to get hungry while I was out.
■ I was afraid that I was going low (hypoglycemic) so I ate (without checking my blood sugar to be sure I really was going low).
■ I didn't want to waste food.
■ I didn't want to find a container for just a small amount of leftovers, so I ate it instead.

Once you recognize how often you eat when you're not physically hungry, think of what you can do instead. (Taking a short walk works for many of them. Eating just a small portion works for some others.)

Eat "One Less"

One less roll, one less pancake, one less meatball . . .

It takes about 15 minutes for our brains to get the message that we've eaten. We often eat a lot of food quickly, while we still feel hungry. Eat one less, and leave the table. You might be surprised to find that what you ate was enough. Many people have lost weight and kept it off not by changing what they eat but just by eating a little less at every meal. And if your "one less" is a starch or sugar, your after-meal blood sugars won't be as high.

"My mindset has changed."

My doctor told me, "It's OK to eat anything you desire, just don't make a pig of yourself. Do it in moderation."

So that's what I do. My control over how much I eat has improved so much, I don't even recognize myself. Before, I'd eat the whole pot of grits, three eggs, five strips of bacon, and two big pieces of toast for breakfast. Now I eat one egg, one slice of bacon, one piece of toast, and a handful of grits. I eat one of everything, and I'm just as happy and full as if I ate a big breakfast.

I found out it doesn't take as much as I thought it did to keep you alive. I take two, three spoonfuls of this or that where I used to take two, three cups!

My mindset has changed. And I had to wait until I was 72 to do that, which is crazy.

— Clarence Donelan

Still Not Losing the Weight

I was diagnosed back in September 2001, and even though I went into denial for the first 6 months or so as my dad was terminally ill at the time, and has since passed away . . . I have totally turned about my diet and even though I don't do as much exercise as I should, I still do a whole bunch more than I ever did. I eat a healthy diet, my A1C results are great, down to 6.5 from 8.5, and my average is 126. Saying this, I should be happy, as my numbers are proof that I am in control of my diabetes, with the help of glucophage, but I am not losing weight very fast. And I have read many others' stories on this forum of people who don't have a problem with weight loss. I have only lost about 10–20 pounds since being diagnosed. I actually attend a weight loss class just so that I can monitor my progress, and luckily I haven't put any on, but HELP, where am I going wrong???? —A

Re: Still Not Losing the Weight

In my own experience I confirm that exercise doesn't necessarily mean weight loss. A good point to remember the exercise will dramatically improve your cardiovascular fitness, and your glucose control even if the apparent benefits aren't seen on the scales. On a more personal note, got a bro- who spends hours in the gym but likes those ribs and cakes and has been fighting the pounds for years. In my own case I was given that generic 1800 calorie diet and had to decrease it 'til I now eat "about" 1200–1500 calories a day. I don't necessarily eat so low each day, which helps keep me satisfied (and feel normal?) as it goes. I lost 95 pounds at one point this way, exercise pretty vigorous. The closer I got to my goals the slower the pounds dropped. In my own illiterate opinion the diet is the most important part of weight loss, being thin doesn't mean a great life with excellent glucose control, and being "pleasantly plump" doesn't indicate poor glucose control or a sad miserable life. It's not for the scales I do this, or a set of numbers, but to have as much fun as I can. —L

Re: Still Not Losing the Weight

Don't know how similar your situation is to mine 5 years ago when diagnosed, but here's what worked for me. I did not even think about weight loss. Only focused on trying to control my blood sugar. Walking for a few minutes after meals and snacks every day is what helped me get my blood sugar in control and has kept it in control for the last 5 years. First two months were on meds, because I had 350 bs when diagnosed, and that, along with the daily exercise after healthy meals and snacks (mostly whole foods in smaller portions than what I had been used to), got me in control within a couple of weeks, and then I didn't need the meds after a couple of months. The pounds started falling off almost right away (a couple of pounds per week at first), and kept on falling off for 6 months until I'd lost total of 40 pounds and got down to normal weight for my height and age (55 at the time). I only wish that I'd known how to do this years before, by focusing on fitness and health (a gain) instead of focusing on losing weight (a loss). Walking is my main exercise (about 90%), but I also use some 4 and 5 pound dumbbells and do a few other resistance exercises as a supplement to the walking. "Fitness" and "Shape" magazines always have some details on these, as well as "fit food." Is your exercise plan anything like that, and have you gotten some good advice on your food plan with the help of a Registered Dietitian? Sounds like you're on the right track, and maybe just need to take it a step or two further. (Possible subliminal message there?) ;) —pw

Re: Still Not Losing the Weight
What kind of exercises are you doing? It is possible that you're losing fat and gaining muscle at the same time. And muscle weighs more than fat does. So, you might actually be doing really good losing fat, but your weight does not go down much because of all the new muscle. I observed this phenomenon myself as my pants got looser but my weight did not drop much. I cannot think of any other explanations. How does your weight loss class instructor explain it? —T

Newly diagnosed

I was diagnosed with type 2 diabetes approximately six weeks ago. My doctor put me on 15mg Actos and gave me the ADA diet and sent me packing. WOW what a shock. I've since been back for one follow up visit and asked the doc for a RX for a blood sugar monitor, I've lost 20 pounds, followed the diet to the letter, feel much better, but my morning readings are still around 150–160. Isn't that too high? The doc said only test once a day, but in reading some of your postings, I think I need to test more often to find out which foods affect me differently, am I right? Will this disease eventually kill me? I actually feel better since I have been diagnosed than I have in a long time. Is that crazy? I'm lost in a sea of information. HELP, a new member to your club. —O

Re: Newly diagnosed

Most doctors send you to a Dietitian that gives you a meal plan made specifically for you. You probably should test more than once a day. Testing will let you and your doctor know if you need to change your medication, diet or exercise. Personally, I would find a new doctor. — J

Re: Newly diagnosed

I have been a type 2 for about 12 years. The first doctor I went to was like yours. I was basically on my own. You need to change to a new doctor. Go to one that knows what is going on. The doctor I go to now sent me to a dietitian/ educator. This is the best bunch of trips I ever made. Most insurance will pay if your doctor sends you. They take the time to explain everything and work with you to maintain good blood sugars. Carbs are to be eaten very carefully. Some people are more sensitive than others to milk, pasta, bread and other stuff. Not to scare you but I am now having to take insulin shots. The pills finally quit working. I feel much better. The dietitian said that most type 2's will finally have to go on insulin. —T

About denial of diabetes

I found out I have Type 2 last August. I don't have really high bs's . . . 140 avg.

I am on Glucophage 850 at nite. I went thru the initial Diabetes class offered by my insurance last year. I have changed some things but not much. I am still way overweight and keep saying I am going to start eating better soon . . . or monday . . . or the next monday . . . or . . . or . . . or. I am with a diff insurance now and they have been really calling me and getting me in to ck levels and get me into another class and keeping tabs on me. I was amazed! Now I hope to "get with it". I need to cook/plan meals/eat better at home and work. Exercise but that seems to be a prob as I am tired all the time. I did just recently start in a water aerobics class twice a week after work. I have a few exercise equip pieces here at home . . . but they sit there. I have even had my friends all test their bs after we have all eaten the same thing just to see if they have high bs levels. they didn't :(sooooooooo time to get real. but how do you start? I just seem to have gotten lazy since my divorce 6 yrs ago. I don't cook . . . as it is just me and easier to go out. I don't go anyplace much due to the fact I have gained so much weight that I cry about the weight I cry about the diabetes. . . . . . . sheeeeeeeeesh I am just not dealing well with it all. it is very overwhelming. I have given it all to the Lord, but I need to do my part too. I don't get on here much but will ck during the week sometime . . . thanks for any advice on how to "get started" God bless you! —RP

Re: About denial of diabetes

I was diagnosed the end of June . . . I have had one heck of a month . . . blood sugars all over the chart. But just this week, they have started to stabilize (still not low enough) between 100 and 120 . . . this is a great improvement for me. . . . and it's been this way for a week now :-). . . . I finally got serious and started keeping a food diary and checking my BS more often so I could see which foods were not for me. . . . Hopefully things will start looking up . . . I really hate this disease . . . My goal is to get off the Glucophage and try to control with diet and exercise. Who knows if I'll be able to do it, but I'm gonna try. I was in denial for nearly 3 years . . . not really officially diagnosed, but highly suspected I had it . . . BS kept creeping up until they finally hit 277 . . . Then I had to admit the whole terrible truth. I think I'm OK with it now . . . but still hate it with a passion. Good Luck. —J2

Re: About denial of diabetes
thanks j2 for your input!! My blood sugars are averaging 140 but are up and down depending on what I eat . . . I think the keeping a food diary is good if I can stick to it . . . I have done them before and get tired of writing things down all the time. but I will either do that or do a menu plan for each day on the weekends to follow during the week. that would be like a diary I think . . . and add to it if I need to . . . but will try to be good and keep it as is. I would like to get off the Glucophage as well. I dont like pills. and now that my blood pressure is up too they want to start me on another pill for that. . . . . . . I see the doc Tuesday and will keep you all posted on that outcome . . . sheeeeeeesh what next? thanks for your thoughts and ideas. —RP

Re: About denial of diabetes

I am 40, and was just diagnosed a couple weeks ago. Last year, before diabetes, I had decided to lose weight and have lost 61 lbs so far. I cringe to think where my blood sugar would be had I not started then. I found it easier to set small goals and look at what I have done right, rather than dwell on what I did wrong. Started out with just today, I will stick to so many calories, then the next day I did too. Whenever I decided to go off my diet, I would think about it some first and see if I really wanted to do that. Sometimes I would feel deprived at some kind of event, but then look at the calendar and see there was another in only three more days ... EVERY day can't really be a special day is what I finally decided. Even though I have a family, I hate to cook. I try to find things that are healthy and now that fit my carbs that are inexpensive and easy. For instance our local supermarket has healthy salads I love. I have found that "splurging" on good deli lunchmeat and cheese isn't too bad after all. I like sandwiches really crunchy, and do

weird things like rolling lettuce (just not iceberg) in a slice of meat so I can get more in it! I found a meal bar that fits my plan and keep those on hand at all times. . . . in fact, I keep one in my purse at all times. If I am out later than planned, or am invited out to eat, I will often eat one of those on the way to the restaurant, and then just a green salad at the restaurant. The key is finding out what works for you. I have listed some things that might seem weird to many people but they are working for me, and I have approval from my dietitian now.
—av

Re: About denial of diabetes

Thanks so much for your suggestions and just talking with me!!! I have an appt with a Nutritionist but can't get in til August. By then tho I will be done with the 4 classes they offer to begin with. She will be helping me to set up a meal plan. but my prob is right now. You know . . . planning and sticking to a diet. I have been on sooooooooo many diets in my life . . . I still have most of the cookbooks for them up in a cupboard!!! But shamefully . . . they work for a while and I do really good at them . . . lose weight. then go off and get back the weight and then some . . . the old "yo-yo" dieting thing. I have been told to not look at this like a diet but as a new way of life. I am making a "schedule" tonite . . . that I will try out this week. Each day listed with what I will do. like what time to get up earlier to exercise, eat, shower, go to work etc etc. . . . I hope to get a new "routine" going for me to include exercise and I will still do the water aerobics twice a week also. keeping in mind small goals and that it will take time to get a "routine" down. I am very impressed with both of your weight losses and your positive attitudes!!! Thanks again !!! — RP

Focus On: Treatment of Obesity

Adapted from "Treatment of Obesity," by Anthony N. Fabricatore, PhD, and Thomas A. Wadden, PhD, *Clinical Diabetes* 21:67–72, 2003.

Most people who have type 2 diabetes are overweight. Losing weight will improve blood glucose levels, blood pressure, and cholesterol levels.

What's the best way for you to lose weight? How aggressive should you and your doctor be?

The National Heart, Lung, and Blood Institute (NHLBI) and the North American Association for the study of Obesity have come up with guidelines for the treatment of obesity. The first questions you and your doctors will ask are: How overweight are you, and how is your weight affecting your health?

How Overweight?

Body mass index (BMI) gives a better picture of whether you're overweight than simple height/weight charts. See the chart on p. 112. If your BMI is 25 or over, you're overweight. Obesity is defined as a BMI of 30 or higher.

How Unhealthy?

Do you have medical conditions that are made worse by being overweight? Such "comorbid conditions" include:

- type 2 diabetes
- high blood pressure
- sleep apnea
- coronary heart disease
- asthma
- osteoarthritis
- high cholesterol

Body Mass Index (BMI) Values

BMI

Height			Weights											Increasing Risk								
	19	20	21	22	23	24	25	26	27	28	29	30	31	32	33	34	35	36	37	38	39	40
										Weight (in pounds)												
4'10"	91	96	100	105	110	115	119	124	129	134	138	143	148	153	158	162	167	172	177	181	186	191
4'11"	94	99	104	109	114	119	124	128	133	138	143	148	153	158	163	168	173	178	183	188	193	198
5'	97	102	107	112	118	123	128	133	138	143	148	153	158	163	168	174	179	184	189	194	199	204
5'1"	100	106	111	116	122	127	132	137	143	148	153	158	164	169	174	180	185	190	195	201	206	211
5'2"	104	109	115	120	126	131	136	142	147	153	158	164	169	175	180	186	191	196	202	207	213	218
5'3"	107	113	118	124	130	135	141	146	152	158	163	169	174	180	186	191	197	203	208	214	220	225
5'4"	110	116	122	128	134	140	145	151	157	163	169	174	180	186	192	197	204	209	215	221	227	232
5'5"	114	120	126	132	138	144	150	156	162	168	174	180	186	192	198	204	210	216	222	228	234	240
5'6"	118	124	130	136	142	148	155	161	167	173	179	186	192	198	204	210	216	223	229	235	241	247
5'7"	121	127	134	140	146	153	159	166	172	178	185	191	198	204	211	217	223	230	236	242	249	255
5'8"	125	131	138	144	151	158	164	171	177	184	190	197	203	210	216	223	230	236	243	249	256	262
5'9"	128	135	142	149	155	162	169	176	182	189	196	203	209	216	223	230	236	243	250	257	263	270
5'10"	132	139	146	153	160	167	174	181	188	195	202	209	216	222	229	236	243	250	257	264	271	278
5'11"	136	143	150	157	165	172	179	186	193	200	208	215	222	229	236	243	250	257	265	272	279	286
6'	140	147	154	162	169	177	184	191	199	206	213	221	228	235	242	250	258	265	272	279	287	294
6'1"	144	151	159	166	174	182	189	197	204	212	219	227	235	242	250	257	265	272	280	288	295	302
6'2"	148	155	163	171	179	186	194	202	210	218	225	233	241	249	256	264	272	280	287	295	303	311
6'3"	152	160	168	176	184	192	200	208	216	224	232	240	248	256	264	272	279	287	295	303	311	319
6'4"	156	164	172	180	189	197	205	213	221	230	238	246	254	263	271	279	287	295	304	312	320	328

BMI >27 are highlighted because health risk escalates rapidly above this level.

What You Can Do

Use diet, exercise, and behavior therapy if your BMI is

- ▨ 30 or higher, or
- ▨ 25 to 29.9 and you have two or more comorbid conditions.

*Low-calorie diets (LCDs)

If your weight is stable now and you then consume 500 to 1,000 fewer calories per day, you'll lose 1 to 2 pounds a week. For most overweight women, this will be a 1,200-calorie diet; for overweight men, women who exercise regularly, and women who weigh more than 165 pounds, it's a 1,200- to 1,600-calorie diet.

In case we haven't said it enough already: We recommend you see a registered dietitian (RD) who has experience with diabetes. Also, tell your diabetes care provider that you're going to be cutting calories. If you take a diabetes medication that can cause hypoglycemia (insulin, a sulfonylurea, or a glitinide), you may be advised to check your blood glucose levels more often. As you lose weight, you may need less diabetes medication.

To find success with a low-calorie diet, you'll need to count calories. Don't trust your guesses! You may be underestimating your intake by 30% to 50%. Your dietitian will show you how to read food labels and measure portions.

Write down everything you eat right after you eat it. The more careful and consistent you are with your records, the more weight you'll lose. You're also more likely to lose weight if you have prescribed, detailed menus. That's another reason to see a registered dietitian.

An easy way to stick to a low-calorie diet is to drink liquid meal replacements (shakes) for two of your meals. Studies show that people who use shakes lose more weight than those eating meals. It's easy to see why. You can't drink "just a little more, I'll make up for it later" with a shake. When it's gone, it's gone.

After you've lost the weight, keep drinking a meal replacement or eating a snack bar for one meal and one snack a day and you're more likely to keep the weight off. One study showed that people who continued with shakes and snack bars maintained a weight loss of 8% (a loss of 20 pounds in a person with a starting weight of 250 pounds) for four years. Those who didn't use that structured plan maintained a loss of only 1.5%.

You can get sugar-free meal replacements, but a recent study showed that regular (with sugar) shakes work fine for people with diabetes. The sugar doesn't appear to be a problem as long as you've significantly reduced your calorie intake.

* Exercise

Exercise is an important part of a weight loss program. However, increasing your exercise without also cutting calories probably will not produce a big weight loss. What exercise does is help you maintain muscle while your diet helps you lose fat. Increased activity also helps you keep the weight off. It also improves insulin sensitivity and improves your heart health.

You'll want to do both "programmed" and "lifestyle" activity. With programmed activity, you know you're exercising. You're at an aerobics class, or you're sweating on a bike ride, or you're with other mall walkers every Monday, Wednesday, and Friday.

Lifestyle activity is part of your everyday life. Make it a habit to take the stairs rather than the elevator, park in the space furthest from the store, and walk to the corner store for a newspaper. Lifestyle activities and programmed activities are equally effective at keeping weight off.

* Behavior Therapy

You know how tough it is to lose weight. Structure and support will help. To increase your chances of success with weight loss, get behavior therapy. Typically, this is done in groups of 10 to 20 people in 60- to 90-minute sessions for 20 to 26 weeks. You'll learn the importance of writing down what you eat and how much you exercise, how to arrange your environment to help you resist and avoid your food triggers, how to stop "feeding your emotions" (eating when you're not hungry but are angry, sad, lonely), how to recognize and correct negative thoughts that sabotage your efforts, and ways to problem solve (what to do on holidays and at parties).

Ask your dietitian for recommendations for a weight loss program that uses behavior therapy. Programs such as Weight Watchers and Jenny Craig use some behavior therapy techniques.

Obesity is a chronic condition that needs on-going treatment. After you lose weight, keep going to behavior therapy sessions. You'll be less likely to regain weight.

More Intensive Options

If your BMI is 30 or higher, or 27 or higher and you have two or more comorbid conditions, and you haven't been able to lose weight with more conservative approaches, you may want to ask your doctor about medication to help you lose weight. Two such medications are approved by the Food and Drug Administration for long-term use.

* Sibutramine (Meridia)

Sibutramine acts on the appetite center of your brain. It makes you feel full with less food. In studies, people who used sibutramine and made intensive lifestyle changes reduced their weight by 10% to 15%.

Sibutramine is not recommended for people with uncontrolled high blood pressure, a history of coronary artery disease, arrhythmias, congestive heart failure, or stroke. It also can't be used with certain antidepressants, such as monoamine oxidase inhibitors or selective serotonin reuptake inhibitors.

* Orlistat (Xenical)

Orlistat blocks the absorption of about one-third of the fat contained in a meal, leading to a loss of 150 to 180 calories per day. Orlistat combined with a low-fat, low-calorie diet leads to average weight losses of 10% of initial weight. And you'll definitely want to eat a low-fat diet, because if you eat more than 20g of fat per meal, or more than 70g of fat per day, you may have oily stools, flatus with discharge, and fecal urgency. (One cup of soft-serve ice cream has 20g of fat. A McDonald's Quarter-pounder with cheese has 30g of fat.)

Keep It Off

The medical community now recognizes obesity as a chronic condition that requires ongoing treatment, just as diabetes, high blood pressure, and high cholesterol levels need ongoing treatment. Your doctor may advise you to keep taking sibutramine or orlistat to maintain your weight loss.

Unfortunately, you'll probably have to pay for anti-obesity medication yourself, at a cost of over $100 per month.

Weight Loss Surgery

Surgery to reduce the size of the stomach (bariatric surgery) is the most intensive treatment for obesity. It's appropriate only for people with BMIs of 40 or higher, or BMIs of 35 or higher plus comorbid conditions.

With vertical banded gastroplasty (VBG), a line of staples is put in the stomach. Food goes into the smaller, top pouch, and you feel full after eating only a small meal. The food eventually moves into the rest of the stomach, where digestion continues, and then the intestines. VBG leads to average weight losses of 25% of starting weight.

Gastric bypass (GB) goes further. Stomach size is reduced, again with staples. In addition, a downstream portion of the small intestine is brought up and attached to the small pouch. Food goes from the small pouch to the intestine. There is less digestion and, because part of the intestine is bypassed, less absorption of food with GB than with VBG. If you eat high-sugar or high-fat foods, you may experience nausea, cramping, and other unpleasant symptoms known collectively as "the dumping syndrome." GB leads to average weight losses of 30%.

A newer, less invasive procedure is adjustable laparoscopic banding, or lap band. An adjustable band is placed around the stomach. Again, you feel full with smaller meals. The lap band can be tightened or loosened. If there are complications, the band can be removed. Weight losses are typically less than seen with VBG or GB.

The screening process for bariatric surgery is rigorous. In addition to the surgeon, you'll likely see a dietitian and a psychologist. You'll be informed of the risks of surgery. One or two patients out of 100 die during or shortly after surgery. You'll be counseled so you have realistic expectations about how much weight you'll lose. Although you may not get down to your "ideal" weight, you'll achieve a much healthier weight. Your diet will be very different from before you had the surgery. You'll be eating several very small, low-fat, low-sugar, high-protein meals every day. You'll need to eat slowly and chew your food thoroughly. You may need to take vitamin and mineral supplements every day.

Despite the risks, bariatric surgery is becoming more common. Some insurance plans cover bariatric surgery when certain criteria are met.

The large weight losses seen after bariatric surgery lead to big improvements in blood pressure, asthma, sleep apnea, and diabetes.

Researchers followed a group of 146 patients with type 2 diabetes for up to 14 years after bariatric surgery; 83% maintained normal blood glucose levels, i.e., their diabetes was cured.

The Power of Movement

Results in One Hour!

Be more physically active, and you will see the results in one hour.

"Baloney," you say? You've exercised before and never lost an ounce? Never achieved abs of steel?

Those aren't the results we're talking about. We're talking about lowering your blood glucose levels.

Sensitivity Training

Your muscles use glucose for energy. When you first start exercising, your body uses glucose that's stored in the muscles and liver. As this runs low, your body looks to blood glucose for fuel. When you're active, more blood flows to the active muscles, and muscle cells can grab lots of glucose as it's floating by. So, during exercise, blood glucose levels fall.

After you stop exercising, your body wants to rebuild the stores of glucose in muscles and liver. It does this by taking glucose from the blood. This transfer of glucose from the bloodstream to muscles goes on for hours after exercise.

That's what happens in the short-term. Being more active every day will lead to long-term changes, too.

You already know your cells need the help of insulin to get glucose inside. They also need glucose transporters: molecules that transport glucose from near the surface of the cell to deep within the cell where the glucose is used for energy.

"Just a little bit."

One day, I took down my drapes. Usually my blood sugar was 120, but just that one day on the ladder made it drop down to the 90s. It proves that exercise is very important. Just a little bit of extra exercise and the body will work for itself.

– Peggy Storm

Glucose transporters are active in muscle cells. Be a more active person and you'll have more transporter activity. More glucose gets shuttled into your cells, even though you have the same amount of insulin in your bloodstream. In other words, you are more sensitive to the insulin that's already there. Your average blood glucose levels will be lower. You may need less medication.

By being more active, you'll also lower your blood pressure and improve your cholesterol levels. Physical activity helps you maintain a weight loss and reduces stress. All these combine to lower your risk of a heart attack.

Everybody's Welcome

Most people with diabetes can embark on a low- to moderate-intensity activity program. Moderate means that you can still carry on a conversation. If you're too out of breath to talk, you're exercising at a high intensity. What's low, moderate, or high intensity depends on how fit you are.

Ask your health care provider to suggest a level of activity for you to start with. If you are very sedentary now, your "prescription" might be something like:

- Step in place for five minutes a day.
- Walk two laps around your sofa every day.
- Walk to the curb to get your mail every day. On Sundays, pass the mailbox and

walk six feet more.

Get inventive with distractions: Step in place during the commercials of your soap opera, or for two songs on the radio.

On days that you're more active, mark it on your calendar in some clear way—perhaps a big, green X. You'll be reminded at a glance whether you've done your activity for the day.

As you get more fit, what was a moderate-intensity activity gets too easy for you. So add distance, intensity, or time. For example, add two minutes to your step-in-place program every week, or step at a faster pace. If you're walking around your neighborhood, walk three houses further, or walk for one more song on your CD player.

Your goal is to slowly increase until you're getting 30 minutes of moderate physical activity on most days of the week.

Many people choose walking. It's convenient (right out your front door), and inexpensive (no membership fee). If you find yourself ducking under low branches and skirting overgrown shrubs, call your home-owner's association or county (try Public Works), and give them the address of the wayward flora. They may send the homeowner a notice, or they may have a policy of cutting back plants that encroach on sidewalks.

If you don't feel safe walking in your neighborhood or the weather is often inhospitable, call the indoor shopping malls in your area. Many malls have Mall Walkers groups. These meet before the mall opens. You can walk alone or with others.

Revving Up

If you're going to increase your activity level a lot, ask your doctor whether you should have a test that measures your heart function while you're exercising hard. Such a graded exercise test (sometimes called a stress test) is recommended if you fit any of the following:

- over 35 years old
- over 25 years old and have had type 2 diabetes for more than 10 years
- have any other risk factor for coronary artery disease
- have proliferative retinopathy or any sign of kidney disease, including microalbuminuria
- have peripheral vascular disease
- have autonomic neuropathy

Every Day

In addition to your "exercise session," add healthy activity throughout your day. Turn your back on labor-saving devices and embrace life-saving methods. Here are some ideas. (Check with your health care provider first.)

- Retire your electric weed-whacker. Use manual shears to trim around your foundation.
- Decline offers by your grocer to help you with your bags.
- Haul your own luggage to your hotel room.
- Walk the golf course. If your course frowns on that, tell them you have a medical need to do so.
- Hang your laundry outside (unless you have pollen allergies).
- Walk your children or grandchildren to or from school. (You might want to start with the walk home—no time pressure.)
- If you can buy a newspaper within walking distance, cancel home delivery. Can't commit? Put in a vacation stop for one week. See how an early morning walk affects your blood glucose levels, your mood, and your alertness.
- Do housework. Help your spouse; cancel the cleaning service.
- Wash your car.
- (Note we're not suggesting that you stop using your TV remote control. We do have certain standards for civilized living.)

Choose hobbies that keep you moving:

- Grow a garden (so you'll have something to weed!).
- Play miniature golf once a week.
- Join a birding group.
- Take dance lessons.
- Call your local park and ask what activities are planned for the month. Do a wildflower walk or park clean-up.

Protecting Your Feet

If you have loss of protective sensation, avoid activities that are hard on your feet, such as treadmill, long walks, jogging, and step exercises. Instead, choose swimming (wear aqua shoes to protect your feet from the rough surfaces), bicycling, rowing, or chair exercises.

Check your feet carefully after exercising for any red spots, blisters, or cuts. Report any problem to your doctor or foot doctor.

Avoiding Hypos

Physical activity lowers blood glucose. If you use a sulfonylurea, a glitinide, or insulin, and you become more active, your blood glucose level could drop too low.

Check your blood glucose levels more often when you start being more active. Ask your doctor or diabetes educator for guidance.

If you're exercising away from home, carry your blood glucose meter and a snack or drink that contains carbohydrate. If you feel that your blood glucose is going low, check first, then treat if needed. Tell your doctor or diabetes educator that your blood glucose went low. If you're trying to lose weight, having to treat frequent hypos doesn't help. You may need a change in your medication plan, such as a lower dose of medication, to prevent lows.

Wear a medical I.D.

FORUM

How long until meds work?

I was on meds for 2 months, then didn't need meds any more. Threw out most of the stuff in my kitchen, and got all new healthier versions. Cut down on portion sizes using measuring cup for everything that could be measured, and increased exercise gradually—walking a few minutes after every meal and snack. My numbers got in control within a week or so. I think meds can help, but they can't do it all.

We have to metabolize ourselves some-what, too, get the heart rate up with some cardio aerobics, and it's good that you're already exercising (I just read your most recent post). Sometimes an adjustment in when, how long, or how hard you exercise can make a big difference. And, if one thing doesn't do the job, try another, such as steps, stairs, biking, ab crunches, push-ups, weights, if you have doctor's permission, of course. I use these little extras in-between occasionally, if I'm away from my treadmill. I think the regular activity throughout the day (and night, too) is what helps the most to get metabolism going and keep it going to reduce insulin resistance. And, it works best for me if I don't do it all at once, but divide it up into several spaced-out peri-ods, morning, afternoon, and night. What I do is check my meter after exercise to see if I'm in goal range, and if not, then I exercise some more. I hope that helps. Let us know! —pw

Re: How long until meds work?
The very best doc I ever went to told me if I wasn't careful he'd put his kids

through college after cutting off both my feet. Now 5 years later, 90 pounds down, pretty consistent diet, real heavy on the exercise, the docs tell me now I'm more healthy than most of their "normal" patients. Took me months to be able to run a mile, and yeah a blue-haired old lady helped me to the bench after hitting my knees. Took me longer to feel as if I'd learn what to do with my meals, and even after all these years I still have failures. Set small goals, learn the food (the library was my best teacher), and do something to get your heart moving. walking? vacuuming? swimming? And each time you feel as if you're not doing it right remember what you were doing a few weeks ago, a few months ago, and 2 years ago. You'll see you're actually doing better. You'll do great, I know it! —S

7

It's Insulin Time

You can't get blood from a turnip, and at some point, your pancreas is simply not able to produce enough insulin for your needs.

It's Insulin Time.

You know you need insulin when your doctor has tried all the ways to use diabetes pills (different pills, combinations, highest doses), but still:

- All your fingerstick results are over 130 mg/dl, or
- Your A1C is over 7% for more than 6 months (two tests in a row)

If your blood sugars are well above normal, you've probably had other signs that you need insulin:

- tired
- getting up at night to go to the bathroom
- depressed
- no energy
- moody
- grouchy

Using insulin will bring your blood sugars back into the healthy range. You'll start to feel better today, and you'll lower your risk of diabetes complications down the road.

There are other reasons you might choose to add or switch to insulin:

- You're pregnant or planning to get pregnant. (Oral agents are not recommended during pregnancy.)
- You can't tolerate the side effects of your diabetes pills.
- You need more flexibility in your diet or lifestyle. (You can learn to adjust your insulin for what and when you eat.)
- You can't afford your diabetes pills.

Join the Crowd

Do you hate the idea of going on insulin? Do you tune out when your doctor says that now you really, really need insulin? Join the crowd.

"My doctor told me I would eventually end up on insulin, but I fought him all the way. I guess I felt that taking insulin would be admitting defeat."

—Marsha A. Vagi

"I considered every additional intervention (oral agents, one shot/day, and multiple shots/day) evidence of my failure to take perfect control of my health."

—Robert I. Selby

"The nurse at the endocrinology department called to tell me that I would have to go on insulin. I thought that was a death sentence. I couldn't stop crying. I felt my life was over."

—Renee A. Jackson

"The doctor finally spoke those words that I was really dreading to hear: insulin shots every day. I didn't want to believe that I was going to have to 'shoot myself up' every day like some druggie."

—Phyllis Stephenson

Does the thought of "the needle" make your mouth go dry? You're not alone.

"My wonderful doctor finally said, 'You are going on insulin!' He made an appointment for me with a diabetes educator. She was very helpful and understanding, but then the moment of truth finally came—at the end of the hour it was time for my first shot. It was about the scariest moment of my life next to childbirth! You know what? It didn't even hurt! I was so surprised I started to cry and said, 'That wasn't nearly as bad as I thought it would be.'"

–Marsha A. Vagi

"I was going to convince the nurse that I could get the sugar levels under control. But when I went into the office the next day, she had all the needles and insulin devices out on the table for me to preview. I was shaking and crying and pleading not to do this. She was very patient with me, but firm, and let me cry for a while and listened about my fear of needles. She then told me to hold the needle and look how small it actually was. I did, but was still not convinced I could go through with it. When she finally convinced me to inject myself, I was shocked. I didn't feel anything."

–Renee A. Jackson

"I'd get the syringe all ready and then sit there for a half hour or so trying to get up the nerve to stick myself. It was terrible! I felt like such a weakling! Finally, my hubby and son laughed at me so much as I would try and get up the nerve to stick myself, that I just started doing it. Humiliation is sometimes a great motivator. Now, it's no big deal, and my blood sugar levels are excellent."

–Phyllis Stephenson

Still resisting? Is your health starting to suffer? You've got company.

"As I struggled to keep my blood sugars down by limiting my food intake, I started to look anorexic. My sisters were so alarmed by my appearance that they insisted we all go to a counselor. During the session, I agreed to make a doctor's appointment to discuss starting insulin. By then, my sugars were very high, and I was feeling horrible. Physically, I was worse off than when I was first diagnosed, and all because of my fear of shots."

—Kimberly Ewbank

"I tested almost 300 mg/dl every morning. I could sleep standing up because the fatigue was overwhelming. I suffered this way for a few years until I became so worried about the terrible way I felt that I just decided to give in and take insulin shots."

—Cheryl Stahr

"My A1C kept rising, and I refused to start insulin. I was terrified of having an insulin reaction and losing control of myself. I stopped smoking, increased my exercise, and decreased my carbohydrates, all to no avail, as my A1C reached 17!"

—Karin Hanson-Sandefur

When you start using insulin, you're going to feel better. You *do* want to join this crowd:

"The change was miraculous. No pain, no thirst, much less fatigue. I could actually put in a day at work and not drag myself home in a stupor. Insulin plus Glucophage has been the answer for me."

—Cheryl Stahr

"After a couple of weeks on insulin I noticed that I was no longer depressed and was feeling better than I had in years. Four shots a day—no problem, as long as I continue feeling this great."

—Wilma N. Shepard

"I couldn't function before I started the insulin regimen. I couldn't process information or remember anything and was morosely depressed. My husband welcomed his wife home that night, remarking that I hadn't 'been there' for about four years. When people asked how I felt on insulin I could only describe it as though I was no longer walking through molasses. What a welcome change!"

—**Karin Hanson-Sandefur**

Starting Insulin

You'll want two people from your diabetes care team working with you as you cross this milestone.

One is your doctor. Tell your doctor you're ready to start. He or she will write a prescription for insulin and syringes.

The second person is a diabetes educator. If you don't already have one, ask your doctor for a referral or find one on your own. A certified diabetes educator will help you conquer your fears, show you the latest injection gadgets, and answer all your questions.

If your blood sugars are high (over 130 mg/dl) but not sky-high (under 200 mg/dl), your body still makes some insulin. It just needs a little boost. A common way to start insulin is:

1) Your doctor tells you which of your diabetes pills you should keep taking.

2) You might start taking one shot of insulin a day, at dinner or bedtime. (Many doctors prefer glargine, a long-acting insulin.) You start with a low dose, perhaps 10 or 15 units. This is usually less than you need, so the risk of a low blood sugar is very low.

3) You'll check your blood sugars more often when you start insulin. You'll want to check every morning before breakfast, and anytime you take insulin. You will be told how to adjust your insulin dose based on the results. Your doctor might give you a chart like this when you start:

If your morning sugar is ____ 3 days in a row:	Increase insulin dose by ____ units.
120–140	4
140–180	6
Over 180	8

When you get to the dose that seems to be working, you might be asked to check your blood sugars at other times, such as before or after meals for a while. This is to make sure your blood sugars are under control all the time. If you're not sure when to check, ask your doctor, diabetes educator, or pharmacist.

More Than One

If many of your blood sugars are over 250 mg/dl, your body is making very little insulin. You need to cover more of your body's needs with injected insulin.

You need a low level of insulin that lasts all day. You also need extra insulin in your system after meals to take care of the glucose from the carbohydrate you eat. (Even if you're not at this point yet, you will be in later years.)

You'll cover your needs by using two insulins with different action times:

■ Onset. The time it takes for insulin to reach the bloodstream and begin lowering blood glucose.
■ Peak. The period when insulin is lowering blood sugars the most. Peaks cover meals.
■ Duration. The total time the insulin lowers blood glucose.

Figure 1. Action of Regular Insulin

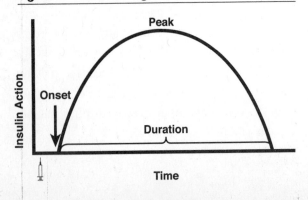

Insulin Type	Onset	Peak (hours)	Duration (hours)
Rapid-acting			
Aspart	Less than 15 minutes	1–2	3–6
Lispro	Less than 15 minutes	1–2	3–6
Short-acting			
Regular	0.5–1 hour	2–3	3–6
Intermediate-acting			
NPH	2–4 hours	4–10	10–16
Long-acting			
Glargine	2–4 hours	Almost flat	Usually over 24
Ultralente	2–4 hours	10–16	18–24

Figure 2. Insulin Levels Before You Had Diabetes

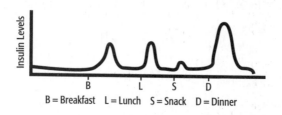

B = Breakfast   L = Lunch   S = Snack   D = Dinner

Figure 3. Insulin Plan: Glargine Plus Rapid-Acting

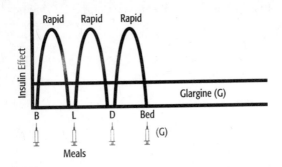

Some Widely Used Insulin Products

Insulin	Manufacturer
Rapid-acting Humalog (lispro) * + NovoLog (aspart) *	Lilly Novo Nordisk
Short-acting (regular) Humulin R Novolin R * + Novolin BR (buffered)	Lilly Novo Nordisk Novo Nordisk
Intermediate-acting Humulin N (NPH) * + Novolin N (NPH) *	Lilly Novo Nordisk
Long-acting Humulin U (ultralente) Lantus (glargine)	Lilly Aventis
Mixtures (% intermediate / % short) Humulin 70/30 + Novolin 70/30 * +	Lilly Novo Nordisk

* Also available in cartridges for pen injectors.
+ Also available in prefilled pens.

If your insulin plan calls for two kinds of insulin, you may be able to mix the insulins in one syringe and take just one shot. Check with your pharmacist.

NPH insulin mixes easily with regular insulin. If need be, you can fill syringes up to a week ahead. You can also mix NPH with aspart or lispro, but you inject the insulins right after you mix them. Glargine (Lantus) can NOT be mixed with any other insulin.

If it fits your insulin needs, you can use pre-mixed insulins. (See Mixtures, chart above.) These are helpful if you have trouble drawing up insulin out of two different bottles.

Insulin Ins and Outs

Store unopened bottles of insulin in the refrigerator when possible. Some types of insulin need to be kept refrigerated after you start using a bottle. Check the instructions that come with your insulin. Injecting cold insulin may bother your skin. Warm a filled syringe by gently rolling it between your hands.

Once you start to use a bottle, the insulin slowly gets weaker. Check the instructions for your insulin. You may need to throw out any unused insulin 28 days after you start to use the vial. If you go through bottles slowly, write the date you first use a new vial on the label.

If you store insulin in a cooler on a trip, make sure the bottle doesn't touch ice or freeze. Insulin spoils if it gets colder than 36°F. Don't let your insulin get hot (such as in the trunk or glove compartment) and don't let it sit in direct sun. Insulin spoils if it gets hotter than 86°F.

Never use insulin that doesn't look right. Regular, lispro, aspart, and glargine insulins are clear liquids. Check for particles or discoloration. Any cloudiness may mean that the insulin is bad. Don't use it.

Other types of insulin are suspensions. There's solid material floating in the liquid. It should look evenly cloudy. If you use NPH, don't use any insulin that has "frosting" inside the bottle or large clumps floating in it. These changes in the insulin mean crystals are forming. This can be caused by too much shaking or by letting the bottle get too hot or too cold.

If you find any of these things wrong with your insulin when you buy it, return it right away. If the problem starts later, try to see if you've stored or handled the insulin the wrong way. If not, talk to your pharmacist.

Injections

Your diabetes educator will show you how and where to inject. You can inject into:

- Abdomen. Anywhere in the abdomen except within an inch of your navel.
- Upper arm. Inject into the outer back

part of the upper arms where there is fatty tissue.

▨ Thighs. Tops and outside. Avoid the inner thighs because rubbing may make the injection site sore.

▨ Buttocks.

The abdomen is usually best. Insulin is absorbed most consistently when it's injected there.

Remember that if you are about to or have been exercising, have a fever, are hot, or have been in a sauna, blood flow to your skin goes up, and absorption could be quicker.

To avoid skin problems, inject at least a finger's width away from your last shot. Don't go back to any one spot for at least a week. Don't inject near moles or scar tissue.

Make sure the spot you use is clean. You don't have to use alcohol to clean your injection site. (Don't wipe the needle with alcohol. This removes the coating that makes the needle go in smoothly.)

You'll buy syringe-needle sets. Today, needles are slim, sharp, and coated to slide into the skin smoothly. Needles come in lengths of 5/16″, 3/8″, and 1/2″. The higher the "gauge" the thinner the needle (30G is thinner than 29G).

Your syringe needs to be large enough to hold your entire dose but small enough that reading the marks is easy. Depending on how much it holds, each line means a different amount of insulin.

- ▓ 1cc: 100 units, each line is 2 units
- ▓ 1/2cc: 50 units, each line is 1 unit
- ▓ 3/10cc: 30 units, each line is 1 unit

Using a syringe more than once is a money saver, and there's no evidence that reusing a clean syringe increases your chance of infection. However, if your skin isn't clean, you are ill or have open wounds on your hands, or you get infections easily, don't risk reusing a syringe. If a needle has touched anything other than clean skin, throw it away.

Each time you use a needle it takes some of the coating off the needle, and the needle gets a little duller, which means it will hurt more each time you inject.

Used syringes are medical waste. Your town or county may have rules about throwing away needles and other medical waste such as lancets. You can buy a device that clips, catches, and keeps the needle. Don't use scissors to clip off needle tips— a flying needle could hurt someone or become lost until someone is stuck with it.

If you don't destroy the needles, recap them if you can do it safely and put them in a "Sharps Container," which you can buy at your local pharmacy. Or put the needle or entire syringe in a non-see-through, heavy-duty plastic or metal container with a screw cap or tight lid. Label the container "MEDICAL WASTE — USED SHARPS." Don't use a container that will allow a needle to break through and possibly stick someone. Seal the lid with strong tape so it won't open by accident. (Yet another use for duct tape.) Place the container in the trash where it will not be confused with recycling.

When traveling, take enough supplies plus a doctor's prescription for syringes and your prescription label. In some states, you may not be able to get your syringes without a prescription. If you run out, the local pharmacist can contact your doctor or pharmacy. If you run into problems, try a hospital emergency room.

Gadgets

Your diabetes educator or pharmacist can show you these gadgets:

Dose gauges help you measure your insulin. Some make a click sound with each 1 to 2 units of insulin, others have Braille or raised numbers.

Needle guides and **vial stabilizers** help you insert the needle into the insulin vial. A few allow you to set your dose with a dial or other device.

Syringe magnifiers make the measure marks on the syringe larger and easier to see.

An **insulin pen** looks like an ink pen. It has a disposable needle instead of a writing point, and an insulin cartridge instead of an ink cartridge. You "dial in" your dose (clicks and a number dial tell you how much you've dialed in), and then inject. These pens are popular because they're convenient and accurate in dose. You don't have to worry about filling syringes ahead of time and carrying them with you. If you're in a dim restaurant, the clicks tell you how much you've drawn up.

Remove pen needles right after use. If you leave the needle in place, insulin can leak out and air can get in, which could contaminate the insulin. You'll probably need to discard any insulin left in the pen after 10 or 14 days once you start to use it. Check the manufacturer's instructions or ask your pharmacist.

Pens cost $35 to $50. Check with your pharmacist or health plan to see if pens are covered. If so, you will need to get a prescription from your doctor. Keep your eyes open for sales.

Do you hate to see the needle? Do you have arthritis or problems holding a syringe steady? An **automatic injector** may be for you. Hold it to your skin, push a button, and the spring-loaded device inserts a needle into your skin almost without you knowing it. Some release the insulin when the needle enters the skin. With others, you press the plunger on the syringe.

After you move up to three or four injections a day, you may want to consider an **insulin pump**. It's a computerized device about the size of a call-beeper that you can wear on your belt or in your pocket. Inside is a two- to three-day supply of insulin. One end of thin plastic tubing is connected to the pump, the other end is inserted under your skin, usually on the abdomen. You change the tubing and the site every two to three days.

The pump delivers a low, steady dose of insulin all day long. This is called the basal rate. Just before you eat, you tell the pump to deliver more insulin to cover the meal. These are called bolus doses. The pump can't decide how much insulin you need, or when you need it—you still have to check your blood sugar, and you'll need to learn how to determine your doses.

Pumps cost about $5,000, and pump supplies cost about $1,500 a year. Most states require insurance companies to cover insulin pumps if your doctor determines it is medically necessary. (Medicare covers insulin pumps for people with type 1 diabetes.)

How-To's

How to Prepare an Insulin Injection

Equipment:

- Sterile syringe. Use the smallest size syringe and needle for your dose and body type. Ask your doctor, diabetes educator, or pharmacist which is best for you.
- Bottle of insulin. Check that the insulin still looks normal.

■ Alcohol swab, if desired, to clean the injection site or the insulin bottle.

1. Wash hands.

2. Choose injection site.

3. Roll the bottle of insulin between your hands and gently turn it upside down a couple of times. (Clear insulins don't need to be rolled.) Don't shake it, because this makes air bubbles in the insulin. Air bubbles interfere with correct measurement of the units of insulin.

4. Wipe the top of the bottle with an alcohol swab, then let the alcohol dry completely.

5. Holding the syringe with the needle pointing up, draw air into it by pulling down on the plunger to the amount that matches your insulin dose.

6. Remove the cap from the needle. Hold the insulin bottle steady on a tabletop, and push the needle straight down into the rubber top on the bottle. Push down on the plunger to inject the air into the insulin bottle.

7. Leave the needle in the bottle and the plunger pushed all the way in while you pick up the bottle and turn it upside down. The point of the needle should be covered by the insulin.

8. Pull the correct amount of insulin into

the syringe by pulling back slowly on the plunger.

9. Check for air bubbles on the inside of the syringe. If you see air bubbles and have not mixed different insulins in the same syringe, keep the bottle upside down and slowly push the plunger up so the insulin goes back into the bottle.

10. Pull down on the plunger to refill the syringe. If necessary, empty and refill until all air bubbles in the syringe are gone.

11. Remove the needle from the bottle after checking again that you have the correct dose.

12. If you need to set the syringe down before giving your injection, recap the needle and lay the syringe on its side. Make sure the needle doesn't touch anything.

How to Mix Insulins

Equipment:

- Sterile disposable syringe, the correct size for the total units of insulin.
- Bottles of each type of insulin you need.

   1. Be clear on the amounts of each insulin and the total units you want. To

find the total units, add the units of short- or rapid-acting insulin to the units of intermediate-acting insulin.

2. Wash your hands.

3. Mix the cloudy insulin by rolling the bottle of insulin between your hands and turning it upside down. Don't shake it because this makes air bubbles in the insulin.

4. Draw air into the syringe equal to the amount of intermediate-acting dose (cloudy).

5. With the bottle upright on a table, inject the air into that bottle. Take out the needle without removing any insulin.

6. Draw air into the syringe equal to the dose of short- or rapid-acting insulin and inject the air into the upright bottle of short-acting insulin.

7. With the needle still in the short-action insulin bottle, turn it upside down so that insulin covers the top of the needle.

8. Pull the correct amount of insulin into the syringe by pulling back on the plunger. If necessary, empty and refill until all air bubbles in the syringe are gone. Remove the syringe.

9. With the bottle of intermediate- or long-acting insulin held upside down, insert the syringe. (You have already

injected the right amount of air into this bottle.)

10. Slowly pull the plunger down to draw in the right dose of intermediate-acting insulin. Remember to draw back to the total units.

11. Don't return any extra insulin back to this bottle. It's now a mixture. Double-check for the correct total amount of insulin. If you drew too much, discard the filled syringe and start over.

Some mixtures need to be used right after they're mixed. If your mixture can be stored, keep the filled syringes capped. Before injection, pull back on the plunger a little and tip the syringe back and forth a few times to remix the insulin. Carefully push the plunger back to its original position, pushing air out of the syringe but not insulin.

(Remember: Glargine insulin can't be mixed with any other insulin.)

How to Inject Insulin

Equipment:

■ filled, sterile syringe

1. Choose an injection site.

2. Use the correct needle for your body type to eliminate the need for pinching the skin. Inject straight in if you have a normal amount of fatty tissue.

3. Push the needle through the skin. Don't rock the syringe. Keep the needle straight to make the injection more comfortable.

4. Slowly (for a count of 3 to 5) push the plunger in to inject the insulin.

5. Wait a few seconds to allow all the insulin to be delivered then pull the needle straight out.

6. Cover the injection site with your finger or a dry cotton ball or gauze and apply slight pressure for 5 to 8 seconds, but don't rub.

7. Write down how much insulin you injected, the time of day, and the site you chose.

If You Reuse Your Syringe

(Disposable syringes were designed for one use only and manufacturers don't recommend reuse. Each time you use a needle it gets duller and may hurt more.)

1. Carefully recap the syringe when you aren't using it.

2. Don't let the needle touch anything but clean skin and your insulin bottle stopper.

If it touches anything else, don't reuse it.

3. Store the used syringe at room temperature.

4. There will always be a tiny, even invisible, amount of insulin left in the syringe and needle. So reuse one syringe with just one type of insulin to avoiding mixing insulins. For this reason, it's not recommended that you reuse syringes in which you have mixed insulins.

5. Don't reuse a needle that is bent or dull. However, just because an injection is painful doesn't mean the needle is dull. You may have hit a nerve ending or have wet alcohol on your skin, if you use alcohol to clean the injection site. Try a different spot. If it still hurts, use a new needle.

6. Don't wipe your needle with alcohol. This removes some of the coating that makes the needle go more smoothly into your skin.

7. When you're finished with a syringe, dispose of it properly according to the laws in your area. Contact the city or county sanitation department for information.

OPEN LETTER TO DOCTORS: HOW LONG IS TOO LONG?

Four years ago, the lab result showed an A1C of 7.7%. I remember reading the note on the printed lab sheet: "The American Diabetes Association recommends the goal of therapy to be A1C results less than 7% and re-evaluation of therapeutic regimens if results are consistently greater than 8%."

I had three years of readings higher than 8%. This year, I had an A1C of 9.7% and felt sicker than when I was first diagnosed 14 years earlier.

Tired, oh so tired, all the time. Everything became a labor of Hercules: getting out of bed, walking up stairs, finishing an afternoon of paperwork at the office. I felt like syrup was running through my veins, which, in a sense, it was—my after-meal blood glucose levels were consistently above 300 mg/dl. My mood deteriorated. I became more irritable and impatient, more likely to snap at my family.

I was the one to broach the subject of being put on insulin three years ago. My family practice physicians responded, almost too quickly I thought, with concerns about low blood glucose. They said that insulin should be a last resort. Fine. But this was a last resort for almost three years. Yes, I should probably have lost more weight, but I was not obese. And the fact is that whatever I "should have done" either wasn't getting done or wasn't working.

How long is too long to try everything else?

Exercise? I exercised like a madman. I'd trained for and successfully completed seven marathons, and I lifted weights three times a week. I was, at that time, at 21% body fat. Too much? Sure. But not obese. I didn't think of myself as a stupid person or just another "noncompliant" diabetic patient.

Medications? At first, I controlled my blood glucose with diet and exercise. This did the job for about three years. When that no longer kept me in range, we added smaller, and then larger, doses of Micronase, until I was taking 20 mg/day. That worked for about four years. Then we added Glucophage, working up to 2,000 mg/day. Finally, we tried Actos. That was of no measurable help to me.

I'm sure that there are plenty of people with type 2 diabetes who don't want to go on shots. Some simply may be afraid of needles. More, I think, feel stigmatized, and they rationalize that somehow their diabetes just can't be that bad if they don't have to take shots.

Uncontrolled type 2 diabetes does all the same bad things as "real diabetes." I use that term to illustrate the mindset of some people with type 2 diabetes, for it was the unarticulated mindset that

I had myself in my early years, especially when I was able to control my disease without oral medications.

But not all people with diabetes think this way. Not all of us are afraid. Please don't act out of accommodating either your patients' resistance or your own beliefs about our being capable of or willing to take on insulin therapy.

Insulin has helped. And I wish that I had started this therapy at least two years ago.

–Ken Sanek
adapted from *Clinical Diabetes* 20:212, 2002

Too High, Too Low

High and Dry: HHS

You're drinking glassful after glassful of water and going to the bathroom a lot. You've never been religious about checking your blood glucose, but as you get sicker, your spouse starts nagging. So for the first time in a week, you check. Your meter doesn't give you a number, just the ominous reading "high." As in "off the charts."

You've developed an acute complication of type 2 diabetes called hyperosmolar hyperglycemic state (HHS). And you'd better be on your way to the hospital, because the combination of severe dehydration and a very high blood glucose level is life-threatening.

Hyperosmolar: The concentration of blood is expressed in units called osmoles. Hyper means high, so hyperosmolar means that the blood is highly concentrated, or too thick.

Hyperglycemic: High blood glucose levels. In HHS, over 600 mg/dl. On average, those hospitalized for HHS have a blood glucose level of over 1,000 mg/dl.

How It Starts

Anyone with type 2 diabetes can develop HHS: people who manage their diabetes with diet and exercise only, those who use diabetes pills, and those who use insulin. Most cases occur in people who don't use insulin, and in people who are over 65.

But HHS is not an everyday thing. Something starts the ball rolling—usually an illness, such as a urinary tract infection, pneumonia, an infection in the foot, a heart attack, or extensive burns.

During an illness or trauma, your body is under stress. This stress causes two things to happen that raise blood glucose levels: Your cells get more resistant to insulin, and your liver produces more glucose. Certain medications raise blood glucose levels, and that may also start things rolling.

If this potential for higher blood glucose isn't taken care of, perhaps with temporary injections of insulin during the illness, your blood glucose will go over 180 mg/dl. At that level, your body makes more urine to try to get rid of the excess glucose. You start to get dehydrated. An illness that causes diarrhea or vomiting is a double-whammy, because you're losing even more fluid.

The process of rising blood glucose levels and increased fluid loss may continue for days or weeks. You'll find yourself needing to urinate many times a day. You'll be very thirsty, but because of the loss of minerals with the urine, you may feel too weak to drink enough fluids. As your condition gets worse, you may stop feeling thirsty, possibly because the thirst center in your brain is affected. You will have a dry, parched mouth and throat, and warm, dry skin (no sweating).

Then you may start acting confused or sleepy. You may have a very high fever (105°F), loss of vision, or hallucinations. HHS is sometimes mistaken for a stroke because some people develop a weakness on one side of the body.

Allowed to continue, the severe dehydration will lead to seizures, coma, and eventually, death.

Treatment

At the hospital, you'll be given insulin to lower the extremely high blood glucose levels.

Even more important than insulin treatment is the replacement of lost fluid. You'll get fluids with a constant drip into a vein. Six quarts may be required, and sometimes more. Amazingly, most people who end up in the hospital with HHS have lost 25% of their total body water.

SIGNS AND SYMPTOMS OF HHS

- Dry, parched mouth
- Warm, dry skin with no sweating
- Extreme thirst (though this may gradually disappear)
- Sleepiness or confusion
- High blood glucose

When you go back home, your doctor may want you to use insulin for a while, even if you didn't use insulin before. Many people are back on their pre-HHS regimen within three months; some are by the time they leave the hospital.

Prevention

Hyperosmolar hyperglycemic state can be prevented. Blood glucose doesn't go from normal to critical levels in a short time—it usually takes days or even several weeks to develop. Therefore, if you're already checking your blood glucose at least once a day, you'll be alerted to high blood glucose levels well before HHS sets in.

Because an illness can make your blood glucose level go up, putting you at risk for HHS, you'll want to take extra care when you're sick.

Opening the Door to HHS

Medications

A large number of medications have been reported to have caused hyperosmolar hyperglycemic state on some occasions. These include:

- glucocorticoids ("steroids")
- diuretic drugs ("water pills")
- phenytoin (Dilantin)
- cimetidine (Tagamet)

● the beta blocker propranolol (Inderal)

Steroids and diuretics raise blood glucose levels. Propranolol may partially suppress insulin release from the pancreas and thereby lead to higher blood glucose levels. Other drugs linked to HHS have no such obvious effects.

Even though these medications have been associated with HHS, that doesn't mean you shouldn't take them. Don't stop taking any prescribed medication without first discussing it with your doctor.

If one of these medications is prescribed for you in the future, it's particularly important that you check your blood glucose levels regularly for the first month you're on the drug. Tell your doctor about any unusual changes in your blood glucose levels.

Treatments

HHS has been known to occur in people having peritoneal dialysis or intravenous feedings because of the large amounts of glucose used. If you're having either of these treatments, monitor your blood glucose levels regularly.

Nursing Homes

About a third of the cases of HHS occur in people living in nursing homes. One of the reasons is that many people in nursing homes lack free access to drinking water. They often have to wait for staff members to offer them something to drink and therefore may get dehydrated.

If a loved one of yours is living in a nursing home and suddenly seems to be doing poorly, consider the possibility of HHS. If the person is more confused than usual or appears to have had a stroke, insist that his or her blood glucose level be tested. People suffering from HHS can look deathly ill, yet fully recover with treatment!

Diabetic Ketoacidosis (DKA)

You know that insulin moves glucose into cells, and the cells use it for energy. When there isn't enough insulin, glucose can't move in, and cells are starved. So the body breaks down fat for energy.

A by-product of the breakdown of fat is ketones. Normally, the body gets rid of ketones in the urine. If they form faster than the body can get rid of them, ketones build up in the blood. Ketones are acidic, and the blood starts to turn acidic. This condition is called diabetic ketoacidosis (DKA).

Normally, people with type 2 diabetes make enough insulin to keep fats from breaking down. But sometimes, people with type 2 diabetes suddenly start making less insulin.

If your body is under stress (an infection, a heart attack), your blood glucose levels will rise. If they're high enough for long enough, the insulin-producing cells of your pancreas shut down. They stop making insulin. This is called glucose toxicity. Then ketones can build up.

The lack of insulin leading to ketones also leads to high blood glucose levels, which leads to excess urination and dehydration, just as in HHS. A build-up of ketones plus dehydration leads to diabetic ketoacidosis (DKA). DKA can lead to coma and death.

Mild DKA can be treated at home with help from your diabetes educator or doctor. People with severe DKA need to be hospitalized. Treatment for DKA, like HHS, is insulin and fluids.

Symptoms of DKA	Signs That Others Might Notice
Nausea and vomiting	Warm, dry skin
Loss of appetite	Rapid breathing; sighing
Abdominal pain	Fruity odor on breath
Thirst	(like Juicy Fruit gum)
Weakness	
Visual disturbances	
Sleepiness	
Urinating a lot	

How to Check for Ketones

You can buy ketone strips at your pharmacy. You don't need a prescription. Don't wait until you're sick to get them. Keep them in your house and check the expiration date every six months.

Check for ketones when:

▣ several blood glucose tests in a day are 240 mg/dl or higher, or

▣ you are sick or feel queasy. Ketones can make you feel sick to your stomach. Don't assume it's just something you ate or a 24-hour stomach flu.

Step 1. Dip a ketone test strip in a urine sample or pass it through the stream of urine.

Step 2. Time the test according to the directions on the package (10 seconds to 2 minutes, depending on the brand).

Step 3. There will be a color change if ketones are present. Compare color to package color chart and record the result. A result of "moderate" or "large" means you don't have enough insulin in your system. Call your doctor.

Sick-Day Guidelines

Before You Get Sick

▣ Discuss sick-day management with your health care provider. Ask your spouse or partner to go with you to this appointment. When all you want to do is lie in bed with the lights off, your spouse may be the one who will keep you from developing HHS or DKA by insisting that you eat, drink, check blood glucose and urine ketones, and call the doctor.

▣ Have on hand sick-day foods such as

sports drinks, regular gelatin, regular soda, and bouillon cubes. Keep them in a shoe box marked HANDS OFF—MY SICK-DAY FOODS with written instructions of what to do when sick and your doctor's phone and pager numbers stuffed inside.

When You Are Sick, Vomiting, or Have an Infection

It may seem that if you aren't eating or you're vomiting, you shouldn't take your diabetes pills or insulin. But even though you aren't eating, your blood glucose may go up because of the stress of the illness. So you do need medication to lower blood glucose.

■ If you take diabetes pills:
- Take your usual dose. If you can't keep the pills down, call your doctor.
- If your blood glucose level is below 70 mg/dl and your diabetes pills can cause hypoglycemia, first eat or drink something with carbohydrate, then call your doctor.
- If you take metformin (Glucophage, Glucovance, Metaglip, Avandamet), call your doctor if you get sick, before taking your metformin. Avoiding metformin when you're sick may prevent a condition called lactic acidosis.

- If you use insulin, you may need to take *more* insulin when you're sick, even if you're not eating much. How much insulin you need will depend on your blood glucose results. Get instructions from your health care provider.

- Check blood glucose and urine ketones at least every two to four hours, until the results are normal. Set your alarm for the middle of the night and check then too, and call your doctor as needed. Don't wait until the morning if ketone or glucose levels are at dangerous levels.

- Call your doctor when:
  - Blood glucose is over 250 mg/dl for more than 6 hours.
  - Blood glucose is over 350 mg/dl even once.
  - Urine ketones are moderate or higher for more than 6 hours.
  - You can't keep down any food or drink for more than 4 hours.
  - You have a fever of over 101.5°F.
  - Illness lasts more than 24 hours.
  - You are dehydrated, have severe abdominal pain, or have other unexplained symptoms.

When you call, be ready to report your blood glucose level, ketone results, temperature, and symptoms. You can often avert HHS or DKA by reversing a moderately high blood glucose level at home. Your health care provider will give you instructions. You may need to take insulin, even if you don't ordinarily use insulin.

▩ If your blood glucose is above 500 mg/dl, you are heading for HHS. *This is an emergency*. Notify your doctor, and have someone drive you right to the hospital. Don't drive yourself—your thinking and reflexes may not be as good as they usually are.

▩ Continue to eat and drink even if you're vomiting, have diarrhea, or your blood glucose level is high. Take in at least 45 to 50 grams of carbohydrate every three to four hours (10g to 15g every hour). The following have 15g carbohydrate:
- 1/2 cup regular soda
- 1 double Popsicle
- 1/2 cup regular gelatin
- 1 cup Gatorade
- 1 cup soup (not milk-based)
- 1/2 cup fruit juice
- 1 slice toast
- 6 soda crackers

▩ To prevent dehydration, drink at least 8 oz (1 cup) of caffeine- and alcohol-free fluid every hour. Fluids with salt, such as sports drinks and broth, are good. If drinking

makes you vomit, drink 1 to 2 tablespoons every 20 minutes or suck on a frozen pop.
■ Rest.

Lows

When there's too much insulin in your system and not enough glucose, your blood glucose level may drop too low. This is called hypoglycemia. It can happen if you use a sulfonylurea or a glitinide, which spur your pancreas to produce insulin, or if you use insulin.

For example, if you take a glitinide and then you don't eat a meal, your blood glucose may go too low.

Do you use insulin? If you make a mistake, for example, you grab your rapid-acting insulin when you think you've grabbed your long-acting insulin, and then you take too much of the rapid-acting insulin, your blood glucose will go too low.

Hypoglycemia is less common in people with type 2 diabetes than in people with type 1 diabetes. People with type 2 diabetes have some ability to recover from hypoglycemia on their own. Their livers release emergency stores of glucose. As the years go on, however, people with type 2 diabetes lose this ability to recover from lows without treatment.

If you take a medication that can cause a low, wear a medical ID at all times. Hypoglycemia is sometimes mistaken for drunkenness.

What's Too Low?

If you're a healthy adult, a blood glucose level below 60 mg/dl is considered too low. Your doctor may set the "safe level" higher if you:

- have trouble knowing when your sugar is low
- have a job where hypoglycemia would be dangerous
- are elderly, especially if you live alone
- have a serious heart problem

If your blood glucose is going too low, or if it's simply dropping fast, your body releases epinephrine (adrenaline). This gives you the symptoms of hypoglycemia. You may feel:

Shaky
Nervous
Sweaty or clammy
Irritable
Impatient
Anxious
Light-headed
A fast heartbeat

Treatment

If you think your blood sugar is too low, check your blood glucose (if you can) to make sure it's really low. If it's low, eat or drink about 15 grams of glucose or other fat-free carbohydrate. (Fat slows the absorption of carbohydrate and adds calories you don't need, so you don't want to eat, say, a chocolate bar.)

Each of these has about 15 grams of carbohydrate:

- 2 to 5 glucose tablets, depending on the brand (this is the best treatment)
- half a can of regular soda
- ½ cup (4 oz) of orange juice
- 5 to 7 LifeSavers
- 10 gumdrops
- 2 large lumps of sugar
- 1 tablespoon of honey or corn syrup
- a tube of Cake Mate decorator gel
- 1 cup of skim milk

Recheck your blood after 15 minutes. If your blood glucose hasn't come up enough, take another 15 grams of carbohydrate and retest in 15 minutes. (Take-15 and wait-15.) After you treat the reaction, if it's the middle of the night or if your next meal is more than an hour away, also eat a snack, such as cheese and crackers.

It's easy to overtreat a low. Symptoms of hypoglycemia often linger after blood glucose levels are back in the normal range. You're scared and shaky, so you keep eating. Then blood sugar will go too high, and you'll have taken in extra calories.

If this happens often, you'll gain weight.

If you have lows regularly, say once or twice a week, report this to your health care team. You don't want to always be chasing lows and gaining weight because of it. A change in your diabetes plan should be able to prevent the lows.

If you take a **sulfonylurea** and have a low, your risk of another low remains high for many hours. Call your health care team. You may be told to check your blood sugars every two hours for 12 to 24 hours.

Alpha-glucosidase inhibitors (acarbose, miglitol) don't cause hypoglycemia. However, if you also take a sulfonylurea, a glitinide, or use insulin, hypoglycemia can occur. In these cases, use pure glucose (tablets or gel) to treat the low. Acarbose and miglitol slow the breakdown of many other carbohydrates, so those carbohydrates won't be effective in treating a low blood sugar.

WEAK AFTER WALKS

Len (not his real name) was recently told he has type 2 diabetes. His doctor prescribed a sulfonylurea. He saw a dietitian and began a lower-calorie diet. He also started walking before lunch four times a week.

He called his health care team with good news and bad news: "I've lost 8 pounds. But my legs get weak and I start to shake every day before lunch."

His health care team suggested he check his blood glucose levels before and after his walks. Within a few days, Len saw a pattern. His blood glucose level was about 130 mg/dl before his walks and about 62 mg/dl after.

"I can't believe what a walk does!" he said.

His doctor cut his sulfonylurea dose in half, and that solved the problem.

GOLF GAME

Marge (not her real name) plays golf after breakfast several times a week. After a change in her insulin plan, she noticed she was going low during her golf games. Her health care team suggested she decrease her breakfast-time, short-acting insulin on days she'll be playing golf. She was no longer troubled by lows.

Severe Hypoglycemia

"Although severe hypoglycemia is rare in patients with type 2 diabetes, fear of hypoglycemia (among patients and providers) remains a major obstacle to achieving [tighter blood] glucose control."

–Christopher Grainger Parkin, MS and Neil Brooks, MD
Clinical Diabetes 20:71–76, 2002

If the early signs and symptoms of hypoglycemia go unnoticed, you could develop severe hypoglycemia. Your brain is not getting enough glucose. You get so drowsy or confused that even if someone hands you juice, you can't drink it. (If they try to force you to drink or eat, you could choke.) With severe hypoglycemia, you can become unconscious or have a convulsion.

Severe hypoglycemia is a real emergency. Someone needs to call 911.

Blood Pressure

"[T]he management of hypertension in diabetes
has become as important and as challenging as the
management of blood glucose."

Philip Raskin, MD
Clinical Diabetes **21: 120–121, 2003**

Most people with type 2 diabetes also have
high blood pressure (hypertension). Lowering
blood pressure lowers your risk of many of the
diabetes complications.

Blood pressure is expressed as two numbers, for example 130/80, or "130 over 80."

The first number is your systolic pressure, the second number is your diastolic pressure.

In the U.K. Prospective Diabetes Study, each 10 point decrease in systolic pressure reduced the risk of

- any diabetes complication by 12%
- death related to diabetes by 15%
- heart attack by 11%
- diabetic kidney and eye disease by 13%

As one researcher put it, "You get a lot of bang for your buck by reducing blood pressure."

Your blood pressure should be checked at all your medical appointments. Ask what it is and write it down in your own health log. You'll be able to see improvement as you start making changes in your lifestyle and take medication.

Guidelines for nonpregnant adults with diabetes:

Systolic (mmHg)	Diastolic (mmHg)	Action Needed:
under 130	under 80	That's the goal.
130–139	80–89	Try lifestyle changes for three months. If still not at goal, start medication.
140 or higher	90 or higher	Lifestyle changes + medication

What You Can Do On Your Own

Lose some excess weight.

Losing just 10 pounds can help lower blood pressure.

Be more active.

Take it easy on the salt.

People with diabetes often have salt-sensitive hypertension. That means that when you cut down on sodium in your diet, your blood pressure will likely go down a bit.

Do you consume too much sodium? The short answer is: Of course! You're American!

Not convinced? Then take this short quiz:

WHERE'S THE SALT?

Do you regularly eat packaged foods?

Do you eat fast food?

Do you add salt when you're cooking?

Do you salt your food at the table?

If you answered yes to those questions, your sodium intake is high.

Some of the foods that are highest in sodium are:

Table salt, or sodium chloride, is 40% sodium by weight.

Processed foods: lunch meats, sausage, hot dogs.

Convenience foods: fast foods, boxed foods (Hamburger Helper, Tuna Helper, mac-n-cheese), canned foods (vegetables, regular soups/bouillon, sauces, canned tuna and salmon, gravy), instant or quick cereals (instant oatmeal), pot pies, frozen dinners, TV dinners, rice/potato mixes (Spanish rice, au gratin potatoes), any mix with a "seasoning" (read: "salt") packet.

Preserved foods: bacon, Canadian bacon, cured or smoked ham, salt pork, pickles, any vegetables pickled with brine.

Sodium is also found in baking soda and baking powder, tomato juice, vegetable juice (unless low-sodium), and buttermilk.

Try to consume 2,400mg sodium or less per day. You learned to like salty foods, and you can learn to like less-salty food.

▪ Don't put a salt shaker on the table.
▪ Cook with powdered herbs and spices instead of salts.
▪ Choose fresh fruits and vegetables, which don't have sodium added.
▪ Read food labels.

Look for foods with less than 400mg sodium per single serving (and then eat only one serving!) or less than 800mg per entrée or convenience meal. Check out the Nutrition Facts of Canned Chicken Alfredo with Pasta on p. 189. It has 940mg sodium per serving. A serving is only half a can, so if you eat the whole can, you get 1,880mg (2×940) of sodium!

PASS ON POTASSIUM?

If you're trying to cut back on salt, you may have been delighted to find salt substitutes, salt alternatives, and "lite" salts in the spice aisle. Many of these are made with potassium chloride. Read the fine print and you'll find a warning: People with diabetes or heart or kidney disease should consult with a physician before using such products.

Why? One reason is because you don't want to use potassium chloride if you're using a potassium-sparing diuretic (for example, Dyazide) or an ACE inhibitor, which also causes retention of potassium in the kidney.

To add flavor to food without using salt, use

- garlic and onion
- lemon zest or lemon juice
- spices
- salt-free seasoning blend, such as Mrs. Dash or McCormick Salt Free spice blends.

Relax.

No, this is not self-indulgent. Relaxation is a very effective tool in the treatment and prevention of high blood pressure. Using simple relaxation techniques, you can produce modest but consistent decreases in blood pressure. For 20 minutes twice a day, do something you enjoy and find relaxing.

- Take a warm bath. Ten minutes will relax you without drying out your skin.
- Take a walk.
- Read a book.
- Practice meditation, learn progressive relaxation or imagery.
- Put music in your life.
- Be sociable. Reach out to other people.

Don't drink too much alcohol.

The American Diabetes Association recommends no more than one drink a day for women, and no more than two drinks a day for men. Drinking more than two drinks a day is associated with high blood pressure. (One drink is 12 oz of beer, 5 oz of wine, or 1.5 oz of hard liquor.)

Quit smoking.

Nicotine constricts your blood vessels. This raises blood pressure and puts a strain on your heart.

Medication

There are many classes of drugs available to treat hypertension. Your doctor will consider your other medical problems when deciding which to prescribe.

- ACE inhibitors, such as captopril, enalapril, lisinopril. Also good for protecting kidney function.
- Angiotensin receptor blocker (ARB). Losartan and irbesartan are ARBs. An ARB may be best if you have kidney problems.
- Beta-blockers, such as atenolol, propranolol.
- Diuretics ("water pills"), such as Lasix or hydrochlorthiazide, (HCTZ).
- Calcium channel blockers.

If you take an ACE inhibitor or ARB, you'll need your kidney function and potassium levels tested periodically.

You will probably need more than one medication to reach your blood pressure goals. If you aren't reaching your goals with three drugs (including a diuretic) or you have advanced kidney disease, ask for a referral to a specialist.

Monitoring

You're taking your medicines as directed, you take yoga for seniors, you've cut down on salt and alcohol . . . Is it working?

You don't have to wait for your next medical appointment to find out. You can check your own blood pressure at home.

You can find many types of home blood pressure monitors at your local pharmacy, durable medical goods store, and discount retailers such as WalMart and Target. Or search the Web under "blood pressure monitors."

If you're willing to inflate the cuff by squeezing a bulb, your hearing is good, and you feel you can learn how to measure your blood pressure by listening with a stethoscope, you'll pay generally less than $30.

If you want to be able to just push a button to have the cuff inflate and you want a digital readout, you'll pay $50 or more. Do you want a wrist style with automatic inflation, memory that stores dozens or hundreds of readings, and a printer that spits out your reading? About $100. Finger style is about $110.

Ask your pharmacist about which monitor is

best for you. If possible have them show you how to use it before you take it home.

Bring your home monitor to your routine health appointments. After the nurse takes your blood pressure, take it yourself with your home monitor, so you can see if your monitor is accurate. If it's not, ask your nurse or diabetes educator to check that you're using the monitor correctly.

Keep a log of your blood pressures and bring it with you to each appointment. This way your health care team will have a better idea of how well your medications are working, because your home monitoring may actually be more accurate than the readings taken in your doctor's office. Some people's blood pressure is higher when it's measured by a doctor or nurse. This is called "white coat hypertension." With a home monitor, you can check your blood pressure when you're relaxed. (Or when you're not. Perhaps you'd like to see how much your blood pressure goes up when you're stressed, like when you have to eat dinner with your deadbeat son-in-law.)

10

Cholesterol

You're born with whistle-clean arteries. By the time you're 2 years old, there are fatty streaks on the inside walls of your arteries, and by the time you're a teenager, there are fatty deposits. Over the years, more fat builds up and hardens into plaque. This puts you at high risk for a heart attack, stroke, and amputation.

A "lipid profile" is a blood test that shows whether you have high levels of certain lipids (fats) in your blood that add to the plaque.

A high level of LDL cholesterol means fat is being added on your artery walls. That's bad. A high triglyceride level is also unhealthy.

In contrast, a high level of HDL cholesterol means fat is being carried to your liver for disposal. That's good.

Lipid Goals for Adults with Diabetes

Diabetes is a "heart attack equivalent." Because you have diabetes, your risk of having a heart attack is just as high as someone who has already had a heart attack.

Therefore, the bar is set high for people with diabetes. Your goals for lipids are the same as for people who have had a heart attack.

Type of Lipid	Goal
LDL ("bad") cholesterol	Under 100 mg/dl
HDL ("good") cholesterol	over 40 mg/dl in men over 50 mg/dl in women
Triglycerides	Under 150 mg/dl

Have a fasting lipid profile done shortly after your diagnosis of diabetes, after blood glucose levels have come down. Just lowering blood glucose may improve lipids.

People with type 2 typically have high triglycerides, low HDL, and normal or slightly high LDL. Your doctor will first target high LDL.

■ If your LDL level is 100 mg/dl or higher, work with a dietitian to lower LDL. This is part of medical nutrition therapy.

If you're seeing a dietitian for help with blood glucose control or weight loss, you're ahead of the game. Your dietitian has probably already recommended a diet that will help lower cholesterol. See below.

■ Be more active.

■ If you have cardiovascular disease (CVD) or peripheral vascular disease (PVD) and your LDL is 100 mg/dl or higher, your doctor may also want to start medication, in addition to medical nutrition therapy (MNT).

■ If you don't have CVD or PVD, you'll probably use medication if your LDL is 130 mg/dl or higher, in addition to MNT.

LDL-lowering Diet

Keep saturated fat to less than 7% of total calories. Saturated fat is found in animal products: meat, milk, cheese, ice cream. Eat fewer animal products, and choose lower-fat versions (nonfat or 1% milk, nonfat yogurt, lean meat).

Ask your doctor or dietitian for your saturated fat limit in grams. If you know your daily calorie count, multiply that number by 0.07, and divide the result by 9. That's your saturated fat limit in grams. Until you get a number, try for less than 15g saturated fat a day. That's 7% of a 2,000 calorie diet.

(If your LDL is less than 100 mg/dl, keep saturated fat to less than 10% of calories.)

Here's an eye-opening Web site: www.nhlbisupport.com/chd1/create.htm You plug in your height and weight, click on the foods you ate today, and the computer will tell you if you went over your saturated fat, sodium, and calorie limits. (If your car is littered with fast-food wrappers and you've got ice cream in your freezer, you can bet you're over on saturated fat.)

Keep dietary cholesterol below 200 mg per day. Dietary cholesterol is found only in animal products. Foods high in cholesterol include organ meats and full-fat dairy products (whole milk, ice cream). An egg has about 200 mg of cholesterol, all in the yolk.

(If your LDL is less than 100 mg/dl, keep dietary cholesterol to less than 300mg per day.)

Where's the Fat?

You can find saturated fat and dietary cholesterol on the Nutrition Facts of packaged food. Note that the Nutrition Facts below are for one serving, so if you eat the whole can (which we're betting most people do), you get 12g of saturated fat and 120mg of cholesterol.

Canned Chicken Alfredo with Pasta

Nutrition Facts
Serving Size 1 cup

Servings

About 2

Amount Per Serving
Calories 250 Calories from Fat 110

Total Fat 12g
  Saturated Fat 6g
Cholesterol 60mg
Sodium 940mg
Total Carbohydrate 24g
  Dietary Fiber 1g
  Sugars 1g
Protein 10g

For nutrition information on fast food or chain restaurants, ask your dietitian or diabetes educator for food guides with this information, ask at the restaurant, or go to the company's Web site (for example, www.dominos.com, www.olivegarden. com). Some examples:

- Burger King Croissan'wich with sausage, egg, and cheese: 14g saturated fat, 170mg cholesterol
- Big Mac: 11g saturated fat, 85mg cholesterol

- Two slices Dominos cheese pizza: 13g saturated fat, 30mg of cholesterol
- 1 cup Ben and Jerry's Brownie Batter ice cream: 20g saturated fat, 140mg cholesterol

Better choices:

- Burger King BK Veggie: 1.5g (yes, less than 2g) saturated fat, 0mg cholesterol
- McDonald's Fruit and Yogurt Parfait: 2g saturated fat, 15mg cholesterol

Keep trans fat low. Oils are liquid at room temperature. Most are heart-healthy. Examples are olive oil and canola oil.

Saturated fats are solid at room temperature. They're bad for your heart. Butter and the fat on meat are saturated.

A process called hydrogenation makes oil more saturated and more solid. Food manufacturers like that, because food products made with hydrogenated oils have a better mouth feel, don't feel oily, and have a longer shelf life.

But during hydrogenation, trans fats are formed. Trans fats, like saturated fats, raise LDL levels.

Food manufacturers must list trans fats on the Nutrition Facts starting January 1, 2006. Trans fats will be listed right under saturated fat.

Some food labels list the amount of trans fat

now. But if you were a food manufacturer and made a product with a lot of unhealthy trans fats, you might wait until the deadline before trumpeting that fact. So until 2006, if you don't see a line for trans fats, you'll want to read the ingredient list. Foods made with partially hydrogenated oil (usually soybean or cottonseed oil), shortening, or margarine have trans fats. Eat less of foods that list partially hydrogenated oil as one of the first three ingredients.

WATCH OUT FOR HYDROGENATED OILS

These frosted strawberry toaster pastries have bad-for-your-heart partially hydrogenated oils in the crust and in the filling. (We've added the bold.)

INGREDIENTS: STRAWBERRY FILLING (SUGAR, HIGH FRUCTOSE CORN SYRUP, STRAWBERRY PUREE, WHEAT FLOUR, APPLES, SALT, **PARTIALLY HYDROGENATED SOYBEAN OIL**, MODIFIED WHEAT STARCH, CORNSTARCH, NATURAL FLAVORS), ENRICHED WHEAT FLOUR, SUGAR, WATER, VEGETABLE SHORTENING (**PARTIALLY HYDROGENATED SOYBEAN AND/OR COTTONSEED OIL**), DEXTROSE.

When Nutrition Facts list trans fats, add together saturated and trans fats. Think of them as "the bad fats." If you have high LDL, keep bad fats to less than 7% of calories.

Likely Trans Fat Carriers
Stick margarine
French fries
Crackers, cookies, chips
Doughnuts
White bread
Muffins
Cereal
Breakfast bars, energy bars
Non-dairy coffee creamer (dry or liquid)

Eat foods with soluble fiber. Bile acids in your small intestine help you digest fat. Your body makes bile acids from cholesterol.

Soluble fiber helps bind bile acids, and then they exit the body in the feces. Your body replaces these bile acids by making more from cholesterol in the body. This helps lower your blood levels of cholesterol.

Good sources of soluble fiber are apples, citrus fruit, beans, peas, and oats. You can also increase soluble fiber in your diet by taking an over-the-counter product such as Metamucil or Benefiber.

Consider using a special margarine that lowers LDL. These margarines have an ingredient that reduces the absorption of cholesterol from the intestine. Brand names are Benacol and Take Control. Check at your grocery store.

Medication to Help Lower LDL

If diet and exercise are not enough to lower your LDL, your doctor will consider adding a cholesterol-lowering medication. For many people, the first choice is a "statin," so called because the generic names end in "statin": atorvastatin, fluvastatin, pravastatin, simvastatin, lovastatin. With the many direct-to-consumer ads, the brand names may sound familiar to you: Lipitor, Lescol, Pravachol, Zocor, Mevacor.

If a statin helps some but not enough, your doctor might add another medication.

To Lower Triglycerides:

- Get good blood glucose control using diet, physical activity, and medication if needed. Triglycerides often come down as blood sugars come down, so be aggressive.
- Lose some excess weight.
- If you drink alcohol, cut down to not more than one drink a day for women, not more than two drinks a day for men.
- If your triglyceride level is over 200 mg/dl, your doctor might consider medication. Medication is more likely if your triglyceride level is over 400 mg/dl.

If it's over 1,000 mg/dl, you're at risk for inflammation of the pancreas. You'll need medication, and you'll need to reduce the fat in your diet to less than 10% of calories.

To Raise HDL:

▣ Get moving. Exercise is the best way to increase your HDL.

▣ Lose some excess weight.

▣ Quit smoking.

If your HDL is still too low, your doctor may consider prescribing a form of niacin for you. It's not the same as taking over-the-counter niacin. The prescription kind is much stronger and it's longer-acting. This helps to reduce side effects, like the flushing feeling many people feel. If you are prescribed niacin and experience the flushing, try taking an aspirin with the niacin. This often reduces the flushing effect.

11

Your Diabetes Care Team

Diabetes is a complex disease, and good diabetes care is a team effort.

You

Diabetes is a self-managed disease. You'll be lab technician (checking blood sugars), doctor (assessing symptoms), dietitian (calculating carbohydrate), and pharmacist (adjusting insulin). You'll need training to play all these roles. An excellent way to start is to attend a diabetes education program. A good diabetes education program will cover:

- Facts about diabetes
- Adjusting psychologically to caring for your diabetes
- Using your family or friends for support
- Understanding your meal plan
- How physical activity helps manage blood glucose
- Checking and recording your blood glucose levels
- Dealing with hyperglycemia and hypoglycemia—their symptoms, causes, and treatments
- Handling minor illnesses
- Preventing or treating long-term complications
- Skin, foot, and dental care
- Using the health care system, including your health care team
- Finding community resources for help with all aspects of diabetes

Look for a program that meets the National Standards for Diabetes Self-Management Education Programs. These programs are recognized by the ADA and have at least a registered dietitian and a registered nurse who have continuing education and experience in both diabetes and counseling. Find programs in your area by calling 1-800-DIABETES (1-800-342-2383). Via the internet go to www.diabetes.org/professional/recognition.

Keep up to date by reading *Diabetes Forecast,* the member's magazine of the American Diabetes Association, or other diabetes care magazine each month.

Primary Care Provider

Look for a family practice practitioner or an internist with experience in caring for people with diabetes. Or you might want to see a doctor who specializes in diabetes—an **endocrinologist.** Your primary care provider might refer you to an endocrinologist when you're first diagnosed, or when you need a change in your diabetes plan, such as when you start using insulin.

The Diabetes Physician Recognition Program, co-sponsored by the American Diabetes Association and the National Committee for Quality Assurance (NCQA), is a voluntary program for doctors who provide care to people with diabetes. Doctors can achieve Recognition by submitting data that demonstrates they are providing quality diabetes care. For a Recognized doctor in your area, call 1-800-DIABETES (1-800-342-2383). Via the internet, go to www.ncqa.org/dprp.

Practicing endocrinologists are listed on the Web at www.aace.com/memsearch.

Certified Diabetes Educator

No diabetes management tool—no new oral agent, insulin, or medical device—is as important as the services of a certified diabetes educator (CDE). This relatively new health care profession has added immeasurably to the provision of good diabetes care.

Christopher D. Saudek, MD
Clinical Diabetes 20:65–66, 2002

Your doctor wants you to monitor your blood glucose and report the results. But who will help you choose a monitor that's best for your needs, teach you how to use it, and what to do with the results? Who will tell you what you should record in your log about exercise and stress?

Who will give you a sick-day plan that includes when you should call your doctor? Whom can you go to when you are fed-up with your blood sugars being out of your goal range?

Your diabetes educator. A certified diabetes educator (CDE) has at least two years and 1,000 hours of experience educating patients in managing their diabetes and needs to pass a certification exam every five years. Nurses, dietitians, pharmacists, doctors, optometrists, psychologists, podiatrists (foot doctors), and exercise physiologists may take the CDE exam.

Diabetes educators work in many settings: in hospitals, doctor's offices, neighborhood clinics, pharmacies, or in their own offices. You could take a class where you'll be able to interact with different educators at different times. Or you might prefer working one-on-one with your educator.

The American Association of Diabetes Educators can provide local referrals. Call 1-800-832-6874. Via the internet, go to www.aadenet.org and click on Find a Diabetes Educator.

Advanced Diabetes Manager

A board certified advanced diabetes manager (BC-ADM) is an advanced practice dietitian, pharmacist, or nurse who holds a master's degree or doctorate and who has passed a certification test. A BC-ADM must have at least 500 hours of experience clinically managing diabetes in the four years before taking the exam. A BC-ADM may also be known as an advanced diabetes management practitioner or an advanced practitioner in diabetes management.

BC-ADMs perform a variety of tasks depending on whether they are dietitians, pharmacists, or nurses. Duties can include adjusting medicines, planning exercise, making diet recommendations, counseling patients, and monitoring and treating complications.

The BC-ADM specialty is new. So far, there are only a few hundred BC-ADMs in the United States.

Dietitian

Your dietitian will teach you how to eat to improve diabetes control, including blood pressure and cholesterol levels. Sessions with a dietitian are so important to the health of a person with diabetes that it's called medical nutrition therapy (MNT).

Look for the initials RD, which stands for registered dietitian. An RD has completed a bachelor's or graduate degree in dietetics or nutrition, gained supervised practice experience, and passed a certification exam. Many states also require a license, so you'll often see the initials LD (licensed dietitian). Some dietitians are also CDEs or BC-ADMs.

The American Dietetic Association (1-800-366-1655, www.eatright.org) can give you names of qualified dietitians in your area. Or ask your primary care doctor or local American Diabetes Association affiliate.

Your first visit with a dietitian generally takes an hour to an hour and a half. Follow-up visits run about 30 minutes or longer, depending on your needs. Follow-up visits allow for progress checks, and adjustments to your meal plan. Your meal plan can be adapted to special goals such as weight loss or reducing dietary fat and sodium, and also to your likes and dislikes, work schedule, and lifestyle.

Dietitians teach you many useful skills: how to use *Exchange Lists for Meal Planning*, how to count carbohydrate, how to read food labels, and how to make healthy food choices when grocery shopping.

Dietitians help you discover a range of nutrition resources, including cookbooks and reference materials, so you can learn how to prepare healthy, delicious, and satisfying meals. They show you how to maintain good blood glucose control even when you eat in restaurants, throw a party, or eat a Thanksgiving feast.

It's a good idea to see your dietitian every six months to a year, or more often if needed. If you answer yes to any of the following questions, then it's time your meal plan was brought up-to-date.

- Has your meal plan been reviewed in the last year?
- Is your diabetes or body weight more difficult to control than usual?
- Are you bored with your meals?
- Have you started an exercise program or changed your medication plan since your

last visit with a dietitian?
▪ Do you want to prevent or have you been diagnosed with high blood pressure, high cholesterol levels, or kidney disease?

Who Pays?

Most states require private insurance policies and managed care plans to include coverage of diabetes self-management training and medical nutrition therapy. Contact your American Diabetes Association by phone (1-800-DIABETES) or the Internet (www.diabetes.org) to see if your state has such a law.

If you have Medicare part B (services outside of the hospital), nutrition counseling is a covered service, but you must go to an RD who is a Medicare provider.

If you have health coverage through a large employer, you may or may not be able to get nutrition counseling covered. Call your health plan and ask if they cover this benefit. Ask if you need a referral from your doctor. Health plans often require a written referral to document "medical necessity." Also ask if there are certain dietitians you must go to in order to have your insurer cover the sessions, and how many sessions they cover.

If you don't have a health plan that covers nutrition counseling or no health plan at all, consider paying for it yourself. Your health is worth it. A nutrition counseling session costs $50 to $150.

Some dietitians offer a package that includes a number of sessions.

Podiatrist

Podiatrists graduate from a college of podiatry with a Doctor of Podiatric Medicine (DPM) degree. They have completed residencies in podiatry and can do surgery and prescribe medicine.

Podiatrists treat disorders of the foot and lower leg. These include corns, bunions, infections, and diabetic foot ulcers. It's a good idea to see a podiatrist before you have a problem. The podiatrist will check the pulses in your feet to see whether you have good circulation. He or she will check to see whether you have nerve damage in your feet. You'll learn whether you're at high risk for a foot ulcer and how to avoid one.

Eye Doctor

You should have a dilated eye exam when you are diagnosed with diabetes and each year after. Optometrists and ophthalmologists do dilated eye exams.

Optometrists are trained in examining the eye for certain problems, such as how well your eyes focus. They are not medical doctors and are not able to prescribe medications in some states.

Ophthalmologists are medical doctors who can treat eye problems both medically and surgically. Retina specialists are ophthalmologists with further training in the diagnosis and treatment of diseases of the retina.

See an ophthalmologist if you, your family doctor, or your optometrist notice any of the following signs:

- Spots, "floaters," or cobwebs in your field of vision; blurred or distorted vision; blind spots; eye pain; persistent redness.
- Loss of your ability to read books or traffic signs, or to distinguish familiar objects.
- Increased pressure within the eye (a warning sign of glaucoma). Some internal medicine and family doctors and most optometrists test for this.
- Any abnormality of the retina. Internists, family practitioners, and optometrists should test for this but should refer retinal problems to ophthalmologists.

Exercise Physiologist

An exercise physiologist can help you select proper exercises, set realistic goals, and stay motivated and disciplined in your exercise routine. A program will be tailored to your health needs. You may want to improve your cardiovascular fitness, lower your blood sugars, lose weight, or develop muscle strength and flexibility. Special exercise programs help you work out even if you are over-weight, have been inactive for a long time, or have arthritis. You should have your primary-care physician approve any exercise program you select.

Look for someone with a master's or doctoral degree in exercise physiology or a licensed health care professional with graduate training in this area. You may want someone certified by the American College of Sports Medicine.

Pharmacist

The specialist you're seeing wrote you a prescription. Will that medication affect your blood glucose levels? When should you check your blood sugar to find out? Will any of the medications you're taking (including over-the-counter remedies) interact with any of your other medications? Are there any side effects? What should you take for a cold when you have diabetes?

Whom do you ask? Your pharmacist.

A registered pharmacist (RPh) has completed five to six years of college, served an internship, and passed a state licensing exam. An RPh can advise you about your medicines and about non-prescription products. Pharmacists now work in doctor's offices, hospitals, clinics, and even well-ness centers.

In the past, pharmacists could pursue either a

bachelor of science (BS) or a doctor of pharmacy (PharmD) degree. After 2005, all new pharmacists will earn PharmD degrees. If your pharmacist is a PharmD it means they have spent a great deal of time learning about diseases and working with patients in a variety of clinical settings.

Your pharmacist is a valuable resource for you and the rest of your diabetes care team. Try to choose a pharmacist who knows about diabetes. You might even find one who is a CDE or is a Certified Disease Manager (CDM) in diabetes.

Ask your doctor or diabetes educator which pharmacy or pharmacist they recommend. After you pick one, stick with it. To give you the best service, your pharmacist needs to keep an accurate, up-to-date profile of your medical history, allergies, and medications. If you move from pharmacy to pharmacy, no one pharmacist will have all the information needed to screen your medication regimens. If you sometimes use another pharmacy, including mail order, be sure to bring a list of everything you take to your local pharmacist.

Ask questions. Whenever you are given a new medication, always ask about possible side effects, when to take your medications, how it could effect your blood sugars, what to do when you miss a dose, and how to store your medications. Your pharmacist might also be able to refer you to other resources in your area for help in managing your diabetes.

Dentist

Diabetes makes you prone to gum disease. High glucose levels make it harder for your mouth to fight infections once they start. And once the infection starts, your blood sugars may go up.

Get your teeth cleaned at your dentist's every six months. Tell the dentist you have diabetes, and ask the dentist or dental hygienist to check your brushing and flossing technique. Beyond regular visits, you should call the dentist if you notice any signs of gum disease, such as bleeding when you floss, or gums that are puffy or sore.

Mental Health Counselor

Depression is more common in people who have diabetes than in those who don't have a chronic illness. Even if you don't suffer from depression, having a chronic disease such as diabetes certainly adds to the stress in your life. You may benefit from seeing a therapist, such as a social worker, family therapist, psychologist, or psychiatrist. This person can help you deal with the personal and emotional aspects of diabetes.

A social worker with a master's degree in social work (MSW), as well as training in individual, group, and family therapy can help you cope with many issues relating to diabetes control, from problems in the family or in work situations to locating resources to help with medical or financial needs.

A clinical psychologist has a master's or doctoral degree in psychology and is trained in individual, group, and family psychology. You might visit a psychologist during a particularly stressful few weeks or months or on a long-term basis to work out more deep-seated problems.

A psychiatrist is a doctor with the medical training to understand how the physical aspects of diabetes can contribute to your psychological health. A psychiatrist can also prescribe medications or hospitalization for emotional problems when needed.

FORUM

How do you know you have found a good doctor?

My doctor isn't comfortable treating diabetes, and the only advice he could give me was to attend an education class. Since then I have been looking for a new doctor. Can anyone tell me is there a list or something out there to help a newly diagnosed person know what it is they need to look for in a doctor who treats diabetes? Maybe questions that you should ask or something? Any help would be appreciated. —K

Re: Good doctor?
"Education Classes" can't hurt . . . especially if your doctor isn't interested. Maybe at the classes, someone can refer you to a doctor who IS comfortable with treating diabetes and who is interested in his patients. I'm absolutely amazed at how many doctors really aren't all that up-to-date on this disease (which by the way, is reaching epidemic proportions in the U.S.). All I can say is to keep looking. . . . ask around, ask other diabetics to recommend someone. —j

Re: Good doctor?
Saw some, fired some, found some . . . I've seen a variety of docs and the best were the "non" specialists. Well actually the absolute best was in a set of med trials where I finally went to these shots. The worst? Another endo who said I was too old for insulin and to lose more weight. The way I found my present doc (changed jobs, changed insurance, changed . . .) was

taking the list from my new HMO to the doc I saw THEN, he went over the specialists who were in that list he knew and recommended, and I called the docs in the same hospitals. I asked a variety of questions like—who adjusted insulin—what standard is considered "tight" control—how often should I test or be tested in his office. Yeah there were more I asked, I crossed the docs off the list, then hired the present. And ironically he admitted never seeing LANTUS in use, BUT is now recommending it because of cute little me. He makes suggestions, allowed me to make recommendations (I knocked him over when I wanted an ACE inhibitor. I now take 10mg a day), and in the end says he can be the lazy one. I guess the doc for me is a tool for my insulins and drugs, I manage my own diabetes care. In your case I'd call a DE (educator) and get a list of docs that you two can go over to find a doc that you could see? —L

Re: Docs?

It does take some work to find a good partner in the mgt of your diabetes— by partner I am referring to physician. I went through 4 endo's before "hiring" the one I use now. To find him I asked friends who are MD's and nurses, I talked to the pharmacist at the drugstore I had been going to for ages, I live in a large urban area with lots of medical/bio firms as well as a medical school. I talked to them. There is a document "standards of care" that your doc should be familiar with—quiz them just as you would if you were holding job interviews. I see myself as an equal with my MD. I suggest things that I have read about, I have told him that his office staff have to stop assuming bad numbers mean non-compliance, and we sometimes go at it regarding my weight (he says I'm fine, my job says I am not—and the doc is not offering me another means of having an income, so . . .) Anyway, the important things are that you feel you can be a partner with the physician, that he is active in the diabetes professional activities (attends seminars and conferences to keep up to date), that he abides by the standards of diabetes care (at a minimum) and if he has a diabetic relative that can be a plus. Sorry for being so wordy—good luck hunting—bag a good one. —kb

Complications

Diabetes complications are health problems that occur only in people with diabetes, or occur more often in people with diabetes. The ones most people think of are kidney disease (nephropathy), diabetic eye disease (retinopathy), nerve damage (neuropathy), and foot ulcers leading to amputation.

Less well known is that people with diabetes are at high risk for heart attack and stroke. Cardiovascular disease is the leading cause of death among people with diabetes.

You can do a lot to lower your chances of

developing complications, starting with the all-important ABCs.

A1C

 A1C is a measure of your overall blood glucose control. The closer your A1C is to the normal (nondiabetic) level, the lower your risk of diabetic eye, kidney, and nerve disease. The UKPDS showed that for every percentage point decrease in A1C (for example, from 8% to 7%), there was a 35% reduction in the risk of diabetic kidney and eye disease. Any improvement in your A1C level lowers your risk. If your A1C is 10% now and you get it down to 9%, you've lowered your risk. If you get it below 7% without too many episodes of hypoglycemia per week, you're doing very well.

Blood Pressure

 High blood pressure increases your risk of heart disease, stroke, and diabetic eye disease. Poorly controlled blood pressure is a major factor in the progression of diabetic kidney disease.

As dangerous as high blood pressure can be, you'll probably have no symptoms. That's why it's called the silent killer.

You want to keep your blood pressure below 130/80. See Chapter 9.

Cholesterol

 People talk about their "cholesterol levels." Doctors call these fats in the blood "lipids." **H**DL cholesterol is **H**ealthy; you want the number **H**igh. LDL cholesterol is bad; you want the number **L**ow. Triglycerides, another type of blood fat, are also bad. You want the level low. See Chapter 10.

Type of Lipid	Goal
LDL ("bad") cholesterol	under 100 mg/dl
HDL ("good") cholesterol	over 40 mg/dl in men over 50 mg/dl in women
Triglycerides	under 150 mg/dl

Keeping your ABCs in the healthy ranges:

- lowers your risk of developing complications
- slows the progression of some complications
- reverses some complications

Everyday Actions You Can Take

Don't smoke. You probably already know that smoking can cause a wide and frightening range of lung disorders. Smoking also raises blood pressure. It damages your heart and circulatory system by narrowing your blood vessels over time. The damage contributes to heart disease, erectile dysfunction, amputation, and kidney disease.

Have you tried to quit? Don't give up! Most smokers quit four times before staying quit. Have you already tried a quit-smoking class, going cold turkey, using nicotine gum or patches? Consider hypnosis or acupuncture. Ask your doctor about bupropion (Zyban). Zyban is a prescription medication that doesn't contain nicotine but can help you quit smoking. You can use it along with nicotine patches or gum.

Eat healthy foods. A healthy meal plan has little saturated fat and cholesterol; lots of whole grains, fruits, and vegetables; and a moderate amount of protein. Eating wisely reduces your risk of cardiovascular disease and some cancers.

Stay active. Regular physical activity helps all three of your ABCs. Need more? Being physically active helps you maintain a healthier weight, strengthens your heart, and reduces stress. See Chapter 6 for more.

Take an aspirin a day.

Take it easy on the salt. Excess sodium may contribute to high blood pressure. Keep your sodium intake below 2,400 mg per day. If you have kidney disease, ask your doctor what your sodium limit is.

Quit smoking. It will make a huge difference in your risk of heart attack.

Watch your alcohol intake. Alcohol can make other medical problems worse. Avoid alcohol if you have:

▨ High blood pressure. Alcohol makes your blood pressure increase. If you already have high blood pressure, cutting out even light alcohol consumption may reduce your blood pressure.

▨ Neuropathy. Alcohol is directly toxic to nerves. If you have peripheral nerve damage in your arms or legs, heavy or regular drinking can increase pain, numbness, and other symptoms. There is some evidence that even regular light drinking (less than two drinks per week) is harmful.

▨ Gastric problems. Alcohol can increase the discomfort of chronic bowel problems such as diabetic diarrhea or constipation.

▨ Retinopathy. Heavy drinking (three or more drinks a day) is associated with the development and progression of eye disease.

▨ High triglycerides. Alcohol affects the clearance of fat from the blood by the liver and encourages the liver to produce more triglycerides. Even moderate amounts of alcohol (two 4-oz. glasses of wine a week) can raise your triglyceride levels.

- Sleep apnea. Alcohol before bed makes apnea worse.
- Other complications. These include liver disease, pancreatitis, some heart or kidney diseases. And, of course, don't drink if you're pregnant.

Curb drug use. Avoid recreational drugs that raise blood pressure, such as cocaine, LSD, and amphetamines. And tobacco.

Take your medications. High blood pressure and high cholesterol don't make you feel bad, so taking medication doesn't make you feel better. You may even have side effects from taking the medications. All in all, it's sometimes hard to keep taking some of the medicines that have been prescribed for you.

- Remind yourself that even though high blood pressure and high cholesterol don't make you feel bad, they are leading you closer to heart attack, stroke, and other complications.
- Keep track of your lab results so you can see that the medications are actually doing you good.

■ If side effects make you want to stop taking your medication, report this to your pharmacist or doctor. You may be able to take another medication that will do the job with fewer side effects.

■ If the cost of the medication is making you skip pills, tell your pharmacist or doctor. You may be able to use a generic version or a less expensive medication. Ask your pharmacist whether the medication you take comes in a higher dose and whether it can be split (some can't be split). Buying one pill and splitting it (you can buy an inexpensive pill splitter) is often less expensive than two pills of the lower dose.

Check your feet every day.

Relax. Doing something you enjoy just 20 minutes twice a day can relieve everyday stress and tension that can contribute to high blood pressure.

Quit smoking. Oh, did we already mention that? Well . . . have you done it yet?

Tests and Treatments for Complications

If you develop a complication, you may have many of the same feelings you had when you were first diagnosed with diabetes: anger, fear, guilt, or denial. You may have thought that you had good diabetes control all figured out, and it's frustrating to find you now have to make another effort. You may feel overwhelmed that on top of the ordinary stresses of life and having diabetes, you have new health problems to contend with.

Treatments for diabetes complications are more effective every year. Don't listen too closely to information about complications from friends or relatives. They may remember therapies from years ago, not modern ones.

The rest of this chapter explains some of the most common complications of diabetes, tests you need to catch problems early, and ways to prevent and treat them.

Your Heart
(Macrovascular Disease)

The flow of blood through your body provides the oxygen, glucose, and other substances needed to run your body and keep its cells alive. If you have high cholesterol, the insides of your large blood vessels get coated with fatty plaque. This is called arteriosclerosis or hardening of the arteries. It limits blood flow. People with diabetes are more likely to develop arteriosclerosis than people who don't have diabetes.

When a clot gets stuck in the narrowed part,

blood flow stops completely, and tissues die. When blood to the brain is stopped, a stroke results. If blood to the heart is slowed for a time, the pain that results is called angina. A complete, long-lasting stoppage of blood is a heart attack.

Heart Health

Do you know someone who has had a heart attack? Did it make him quit his 30-year smoking habit? Did she join an exercise program at the hospital and now feels better than she has in years?

If you had a heart attack, would you finally make good on all your promises to eat right, lose a little weight, quit smoking, and be more active?

Consider it done. Diabetes is equal to a first heart attack in terms of the damage to your heart. Your risk of having a heart attack is as high as someone who has already suffered a heart attack.

So sit back, close your eyes, and really think: What would I do differently if this were my first day home from the hospital after a heart attack?

You already know much of what you need to do. Remind yourself every day that it's *four times* as important for you to take all those steps toward a heart-healthy lifestyle, because people with diabetes have up to *four times* the risk of a heart attack as someone who doesn't have diabetes. Though heart attacks are often thought of as a men's problem, women with diabetes have the same risk as men.

If It Happens

Because you're at high risk of a heart attack, you'll want to be prepared to minimize the damage if you do have a heart attack.

■ Know the symptoms of a heart attack.
    You may have only one or two of these. They'll last more than a few minutes or come and go.
- Pain in your chest area, spreading to your left shoulder, arm, and jaw. This is the classic symptom, but diabetes may have damaged the nerves in your chest, so you might not have chest pain.
- Chest tightness or pressure (like an elephant is sitting on your chest).
- Stomach pain.
- A feeling of indigestion. Don't take an antacid and hope the burning in your chest goes away.
- Shortness of breath.
- Nausea, vomiting.
- Cold sweats.
- A feeling of dread, unexplained anxiety.
- Lightheadedness, fainting.
- Unexplained weakness or fatigue.
- Sudden out-of-control blood sugars.

■ Have your family members read the above symptoms. Here are other signs they may notice in you:

- Keeps moving around, can't seem to get comfortable.
- Face is gray or pale.
- Suddenly looks older.
- Denial. A person having a heart attack often tells other people about the symptoms but denies that it's a heart attack, even if he or she has had a heart attack before. Be prepared to hear: "It's nothing, I just need to rest." "Stop fussing, it's just heartburn . . . a pulled muscle . . . bronchitis . . . the flu." "It's not a heart attack!"

■ Don't wait more than five minutes after your symptoms start before calling 911.

Don't call your own doctor for advice. This will waste precious time. You need to get to the hospital within one hour of the first symptoms of a heart attack to have the best chance of survival.

Don't drive yourself to the hospital, because you might pass out while you're driving. Don't have a friend drive you, because once you get to the hospital, you'll have to take time to describe your symptoms. When you're brought by ambulance, the EMTs start treating you right away and call ahead to the hospital.

▮ Buy a small package of uncoated, adult-strength aspirin.

Make sure everyone in your house knows where it is. When you have symptoms of a heart attack, first call 911. Then chew an uncoated aspirin and drink water. If all you have is coated aspirin, have someone crush it and put it in water, then drink that. Aspirin helps slow the formation of blood clots and helps dissolve them. This lessens the damage to your heart. When you get to the hospital, you'll be given stronger drugs that dissolve blood clots.

FORUM

Smoking

 I'm having a problem with the cigarettes too . . . but am trying . . . one thing I know for sure, smoking is BAD BAD BAD for many reasons. . . . One article I recently read (and I'm reading a lot these days) states, "if you smoke, you're just asking for amputation" . . . pretty scary. –j2

Re: Smoking

I smoked for 30 yrs and quit cold turkey 1½ yrs ago . . . then about a year ago I find out I have type 2 . . . sheeeeeeeesh I

wanted to just pick up the cigs again . . .
I still do sometimes, but think of how
much better off I am without them . . .
—RP

Re: Smoking
Never give up on the cigarette thing. It
was, without a doubt, the hardest thing
I ever did, and without a doubt the best
thing I ever did, and my greatest accom-
plishment. (Not to under-emphasize the
importance.) —w

Stroke

Diabetes increases your risk of "ischemic"
(caused by a blocked blood vessel) stroke. The
signs of a stroke are:

- Sudden weakness or numbness of the face,
  arm, or leg on one side of the body
- Sudden dimness or loss of vision, particularly in one eye
- Trouble talking or understanding speech
- Unexplained dizziness, unsteadiness, or
  sudden falls
- Sudden, severe headache with no apparent
  cause

If you have one or more of these symptoms, call
911.

"Make the Link! Diabetes, Heart Disease, and Stroke" is an initiative of the American Diabetes Association and the American College of Cardiology aimed at increasing awareness of the link between diabetes and heart disease. Go to: www.diabetes. org/main/info/link.jsp

Focus On: An Aspirin a Day

The first step toward a heart attack or stroke is the narrowing of a major artery. This takes years to develop. The second step is much quicker: A blood clot forms and blocks the narrow opening, completely stopping the flow of blood. Heart muscle or brain tissue begins to die.

The blood of people with type 2 diabetes clots more easily than normal, which is one reason they have such a high risk of heart attack and stroke.

Aspirin makes it harder for blood to clot, so taking an aspirin a day lowers your risk of a heart attack or stroke. The American Diabetes Association recommends that most adults with diabetes take an aspirin a day. Specifically:

■ The American Diabetes Association recommends a daily aspirin for men and women who have signs of large vessel disease. This includes those who have had one or more of the following:

- heart attack
- vascular bypass surgery
- stroke or transient ischemic attack (TIAs or "mini-strokes")
- peripheral vascular disease
- claudication (pain in calves when walking)
- angina (short-lived chest pain that occurs during physical or emotional exertion)

■ Aspirin should also be used in men and women who (one or more of the following):

- are over 40 years old
- have a family history of heart disease
- smoke
- have high blood pressure
- have protein in the urine
- have unhealthy lipid levels

The recommended dose is 75–162mg per day. Ask your doctor what dose you should take. (Remember that Tylenol and Advil don't contain aspirin.)

To reduce stomach upset:

■ take aspirin with food
■ use enteric-coated aspirin

Your doctor may advise you *not* to take aspirin if you:

▓ have ulcers or liver disease
▓ already take a blood thinner
▓ are allergic to aspirin
▓ have a bleeding disorder
▓ use a medication that might be affected by aspirin
▓ are under age 21

Your Eyes (Retinopathy)

▓ Up to 21% of people newly diagnosed with type 2 diabetes have retinopathy.
▓ Over 60% of people who have had type 2 diabetes for 20 years have retinopathy.

Retinopathy and nephropathy are called microvascular complications, because they spring from problems with the tiniest blood vessels.

Retinopathy is a disease of the tiny blood vessels that supply the retinas, the "movie screens" at the back of your eyes where the images you see are projected. When it begins, you don't notice diabetic retinopathy. It takes an exam by an eye doctor to see the changes in the blood vessels. Detected early, retinopathy can be slowed or stopped altogether.

In one form of diabetic retinopathy, blood vessels may close off or weaken and leak blood, fluid, and fat into the eye. This form is called nonproliferative (background) retinopathy. It may lead to blurry vision, but it usually does not cause blindness.

Nonproliferative retinopathy can progress to a more serious, rarer condition called proliferative retinopathy. When this happens, new blood vessels sprout in the retina. That may sound good, but the new vessels grow out of control. They are fragile, so they rupture easily with high blood pressure, exercise, vomiting from morning sickness, or even while sleeping. Blood may leak into the fluid-filled portion of the eye in front of the retina, impairing sight. Scar tissue may form on the retina as well. When the scar tissue shrinks, it can pull the retinal layers apart. This damages sight; images look as though they are projected on a sheet flapping in the breeze.

Glaucoma may go along with proliferative retinopathy. This increased pressure in the eye can be treated if it is spotted early on.

Retinopathy can also affect the macula of the eye, the central portion of the retina that gives you sharp vision for seeing fine detail. The swelling of the macula, called macular edema, can limit vision and lead to blindness.

Catch It Early

 Long before vision is affected by diabetes, tiny changes occur in the retina. If these changes are caught early, they can be treated so that your vision isn't affected.

Your primary care physician will look into your eyes during your yearly physical exams, but you also need a more thorough exam by an eye doctor—an ophthalmologist or an optometrist. You need a **dilated eye exam.** It goes like this:

The eye doctor puts drops in your eyes to dilate (open up) your pupils. You're sent back to the waiting room. You'll start to have trouble focusing. For example, you may not be able to read the magazine that you had been reading just before you got the drops. After about a half an hour, you're brought back into the exam room and the doctor uses a strong light to look into your eyes and examine your retinas.

When you're leaving the office, because your pupils are dilated, you'll be told to wear sunglasses on the way home. If you don't have any, you may be given disposable sunglasses.

If the above description doesn't sound familiar to you, you have not had a dilated eye exam. Make an appointment with an eye doctor today. Don't wait for your primary care doctor to suggest it. Studies show that many doctors fail to remind their patients with diabetes to have eye exams. And don't wait until you have trouble with your eyes. You can have severe, sight-threatening changes in your retinas without having any symptoms.

	Have first dilated eye exam:	Minimum routine follow-up:
Type 2 diabetes	At diagnosis of diabetes	Yearly

Treatment

The best treatment for people with diabetes in danger of losing their sight involves a laser—an intense beam of light. An ophthalmologist aims the laser at the retina to create hundreds of tiny burns that destroy abnormal blood vessels, patch leaky ones, and slow the formation of new fragile vessels. This procedure is called photocoagulation. In people with high-risk proliferative retinopathy or macular edema, photocoagulation can usually prevent blindness.

Photocoagulation may not work if the retina has bled a lot or has detached. In these cases, surgery called vitrectomy can remove the blood and scar tissue, stop bleeding, replace some of the vitreous (the clear, jelly-like fluid in the eye) with salt solution, and repair the detached retina.

If you need either of these procedures, choose an ophthalmologist who specializes in retinal disease and has patients with diabetes.

And remember that the earlier the procedure is done, the better.

If laser treatment or vitrectomy fail to restore vision, low-vision aids can often help people regain the ability to read the paper, do paperwork, or watch TV.

If you have retinopathy, discuss your exercise program with your eye doctor. Some activities can raise the pressure inside your eyes and lead to bleeding in the retina.

Your Kidneys (Nephropathy)

Your kidneys work 24 hours a day to cleanse your blood of toxic substances made by or taken into the body. These toxins enter the kidney by crossing the walls of small blood vessels, the capillaries, that border it. In people with nephropathy, these capillaries stop being good filters. They become blocked and leakier at the same time. As a result, some wastes that should be removed stay in the blood, and some protein that should stay in the blood is removed and lost in the urine.

Progression

In the early stages of kidney disease, very small amounts of protein leak into the urine. This condition is called microalbuminuria (micro = small, albumin = protein, uria = urine). It's one of the earliest stages of kidney disease that can be detected. Some people have microalbuminuria when they are diagnosed with type 2 diabetes, which is a sign that they've actually had diabetes for a number of years.

Several years after a person has microalbuminuria (mi-cro-al-byu-min-UR-i-a), the kidneys begin to spill larger amounts of protein. At this point, the person is said to have clinical proteinuria and overt nephropathy.

As damage to the filters increases, poisons that are normally removed by the kidneys build up in the blood.

Catch It Early

 If you know you have microalbuminuria, you and your doctor can take steps to slow the progression.

You should be tested for microalbuminuria every year, starting when you are diagnosed with type 2 diabetes.

Your doctor may have already tested you for proteinuria. This can be done with a standard urine dipstick test in your doctor's office. If the test is negative, you should have the more sensitive test that can detect microalbuminuria.

Your doctor can screen for microalbuminuria

by testing a sample of your urine in the office. The ratio of albumin to creatinine (a waste product) is determined. Normal is less than 30 mg albumin per 1 gram creatinine.

Your doctor might ask you to collect your urine for a certain amount of time: for 4 hours, or overnight, or for 24 hours. It is then tested. Normal is less than 30 mg albumin in 24 hours; microalbuminuria is 30 to 300 mg; proteinuria is more than 300 mg.

Other stresses to your body, such as an infection or fever, may cause the test to be positive. Therefore, if one test is positive, you will be retested. If two out of three tests in three to six months are positive, then you know you have microalbuminuria, and treatment should be started.

If you haven't been tested for microalbuminuria, the next time you see your doctor, arrange to have it done. Don't wait for your doctor to bring it up. In a survey of 1,000 primary care doctors, almost half did not test their patients with diabetes for microalbuminuria.

Treatments

If you are found to have microalbuminuria, you and your doctor will redouble efforts to get your blood pressure and blood glucose levels down. You may be prescribed a blood pressure medication shown to preserve kidney function:

either an ACE inhibitor or an angiotensin receptor blocker (ARB).

You may be advised to lower the amount of protein in your diet.

Very advanced kidney disease means that filtration is greatly disrupted and the kidneys are failing. This condition is end stage renal disease. At this point, there are only two treatment options: dialysis and kidney transplantation.

Your Nerves (Neuropathy)

Too much blood glucose damages the nervous system. Damaged nerves either can't send messages, send them at the wrong time, or send them too slowly. (The brain and spinal cord are not affected.)

Researchers still aren't sure why high blood glucose harms nerves. It's possible that glucose-coated proteins damage nerves, or high levels of glucose may upset the chemical balance inside nerves. The damage can be indirect, if the blood supply to the nerves is limited and nerves don't receive enough oxygen.

Peripheral   neuropathy   with   pain. Neuropathy can strike nerves in the hands and feet. You may feel shooting or stabbing pains, burning, tingling or prickling, or weakness.

Treatment. The pain of peripheral neuropathy will often vanish after a few months or a year of good blood glucose control. Your doctor can prescribe various medications that may relieve pain. These include antidepressants and antiepileptic drugs. A cream made from an extract of hot peppers may work for people who don't respond to other treatments.

Peripheral neuropathy with numbness. See Foot Problems.

Focal neuropathy. A rarer condition, focal neuropathy centers on a single nerve or group of nerves. It may arise when blood supply to a nerve shuts off because a vessel becomes blocked. It may also happen when a nerve becomes squeezed. It can injure nerves that sense touch and pain as well as nerves responsible for moving muscles. Fortunately, it usually goes away fairly fast, within two weeks to 18 months, after better blood glucose control is achieved.

Carpal tunnel syndrome is one focal neuropathy seen more often in people with diabetes. The median nerve of the forearm can be squeezed in its passageway, or tunnel, by the carpal bones at the wrist. The syndrome is three times more common in women than in men. It may cause tingling, burning, and numbness so that you may drop objects. Fortunately, carpal tunnel syndrome is not permanent. You can treat it with good blood glucose control, medications, or surgery to remove tissues squeezing the nerve.

Autonomic neuropathy. Neuropathy can damage nerves that you don't control voluntarily, such as those to your internal organs. This condition is called autonomic neuropathy. It may slow down stomach and gut muscles, leading to constipation, a feeling of fullness, diarrhea, nausea, or occasional vomiting.

Damaged nerves to the bladder may cause muscle weakness so that it can't get completely empty. Then the bladder will occasionally empty involuntarily. Because urine remains in the bladder for a long time, it can cause urinary tract infections.

Men may slowly lose the ability to have an erection, even though they still have sexual desire (see Erectile Dysfunction below). Women, too, may have decreased sexual response.

Nerves that control blood pressure may be affected; when you stand up, you may feel dizzy or lightheaded. Your nurse can test for this by checking your blood pressure when you're lying down and when you stand up.

Nerves to the skin may cause too much or too little sweating or very dry skin.

Nerves to the heart may fail to speed up or slow down your heart rate in response to exercise. This is one reason to get a check-up before you begin any exercise program. If you can't trust your heart rate to reflect your exertion, you won't be able to use standard ways to find target heart rate during and after a workout.

Treatment

There are different treatments for the different effects of autonomic neuropathy. Digestive problems take patience and some trial and error to treat. You may be able to avoid them by changing your eating habits. Eat small, frequent meals instead of large ones, and choose lower-fiber foods. Some medications can increase emptying of gut and eliminate the feeling of fullness.

Incontinence, or urine leakage, can be treated with training in bladder control and timed urination by a planned bladder-emptying program. Urinate by the clock every two hours rather than waiting for the feeling of fullness. Men may need to urinate sitting down. Applying pressure over the bladder may be helpful. If these steps don't work, taking oral medications, learning to use a catheter, and having surgery can work. Fecal incontinence (passing stool involuntarily) is treated with medicine for diarrhea and biofeedback training.

Sudden drops in blood pressure on standing can

be treated as well. You may need to stop drinking alcohol. Your doctor may have you stop taking certain medications, such as diuretics. Your doctor may prescribe a medication for low blood pressure, and may advise you to raise the salt content of your diet, change your sleeping position, and improve your general health. Be careful when you stand up, and try not to stand still for long periods of time to prevent fainting. When you get up in the morning, sit on the edge of the bed and dangle your feet for five minutes before you stand up.

Your Sex Life (Erectile Dysfunction)

Erectile dysfunction (impotence) occurs in over half of men over age 50 who have diabetes. It can affect younger men as well.

Diabetes and the metabolic syndrome damages nerves and blood vessels. When the nerves are damaged, small blood vessels don't relax, which prevents them from expanding with the flow of blood that makes the penis erect. Rarely, erectile dysfunction occurs when blood vessels are blocked or made narrow because of vascular disease.

Some drugs used to treat high blood pressure, anxiety, depression, peptic ulcers, and painful neuropathy may cause erectile dysfunction in some men. If you take any of these types of drugs and experience erectile dysfunction, tell your doctor. You may be able to switch to a different medication.

Erectile dysfunction is a treatable problem. Because there are many causes and many different treatments, your case needs to be assessed individually. If you're experiencing erectile dysfunction, you'll want to have a complete exam before any treatment is started. You may want to see a urologist.

Treatments

Oral medication. Sildenafil (Viagra) is a pill that can help with erectile dysfunction. About 60% to 70% of men with erectile dysfunction respond to sildenafil.

Penile constriction ring. This works for men who can get erections but have problems maintaining them. After you get an erection, you put the constriction ring at the base of your penis and take it off after you've had intercourse.

Vacuum erection. You put the plastic tube over your penis. With a hand- or battery-operated pump, you create a vacuum within the tube. This draws blood into your penis, resulting in an erection. You then put a constriction ring at the base of your penis to trap the blood.

These devices are quite safe and relatively successful. However, they do require a moderate amount of manual dexterity, and some couples find them to be intrusive.

The MUSE System. Using a small plunger device, you insert a small pellet of medication directly into your urethra. The medication—prostaglandin—causes the arteries of the penis to relax. More blood flows into the penis, causing an erection.

Penile self-injection. Using a fine needle, you inject a small amount of medication directly into your penis. The medication causes the blood vessels to expand, bringing extra blood into the penis and causing an erection.

Penile prostheses. One type is a semi-rigid, bendable rod that is surgically implanted into the penis. Another type is a more complex mechanical system of inflatable cylinders. When an erection is needed, the cylinders are inflated with a pump placed within the scrotum.

These prostheses have become less popular of late. There is a risk of infection and equipment breakdown. When prosthesis malfunction occurs, it usually requires surgical correction.

Your Feet

If you ever see a talk by a foot doctor, you'll likely see a slide of "things found in patients' shoes." The odd assortment may include a key, a paper clip, a tack, a pebble, a coin. These are some of the items that people with diabetes have had in their shoes that they couldn't feel. They walked around all day and never felt the items grinding into their skin. Why not? They had lost "protective sensation."

High blood glucose levels lead to nerve damage. When the small nerves in your feet are affected, you lose some sensation. You can't feel when bath water is too hot, you can't feel a paper clip in your shoe, you can't feel when your shoes are too tight and a blister is forming. (Oddly, with nerve damage, you may have unwanted "pins and needles" sensations and still have loss of protective sensation.)

Unrelieved pressure or friction can lead to damage to the skin, which is often the first step on the road to a foot ulcer that could lead to amputation.

Even if you were recently diagnosed with diabetes, you may have loss of protective sensation. Remember that type 2 diabetes typically goes undiagnosed for eight to ten years. That's long enough for nerve damage to develop.

Catch It Early

 If you know you have lost protective sensation, you'll know to be extra careful about your feet. You'll check your feet every day for irritations. You'll wear good athletic shoes rather than tight, pointy-toed shoes that may give you blisters.

You'll have a health care professional examine your feet every three months.

Your doctor can test you for **loss of protective sensation** by using what's called a monofilament. It looks like a long bristle from a paint brush. Your doctor touches it to various places on the bottom of your foot. If you can't feel the touch, you have lost protective sensation.

Monofilament testing should be part of a yearly exam of your feet. If your doctor or nurse hasn't tested you and doesn't seem to know what you're talking about, you can get your own monofilament for free and have a family member test you. Call Health Resources and Services Administration at 1-888-ASK-HRSA   (1-888-275-4772).   Or go to the Lower Extremity Amputation Prevention Program Web site at bphc.hrsa.gov/leap

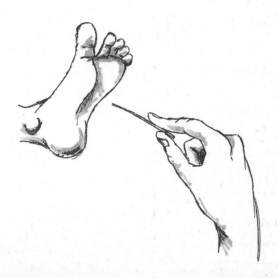

Next Step: Slow Healing

Before you developed diabetes, a blister or tiny cut on your foot would have been no big deal. Take the shoe off, let the body heal itself.

Not so now. Diabetes damages blood vessels. When the vessels in and leading to your feet are damaged, it's called **peripheral vascular disease** (PVD) or peripheral arterial disease (PAD). It's another form of macrovascular disease.

If you have PVD, you have poor circulation in your feet. Less oxygen-carrying blood gets to the skin of your feet, and healing will be slow. That leaves more time for an infection to take hold. Left untreated, the infected cut will probably get worse, turn into a hard-to-heal ulcer, and could lead to amputation.

Symptoms of PVD are:

- Tightness or pain in your leg when you walk even short distances or climb stairs, or not being able to walk as far or as fast as you used to. Don't just brush such symptoms off as normal aches of aging—tell your doctor.
- Cold feet.
- Toes that look red or blue.
- Hair loss on the toes.
- Shiny skin on feet and lower legs.

To check for poor circulation, your doctor will feel

for pulses on top of your foot and behind your inner ankle bone. Special tests may be done to help your doctor listen to and record the flow of blood or delivery of oxygen to your feet and legs.

If these simple tests show evidence of PVD, you'll be referred to a vascular surgeon. He or she may order an X-ray called an arteriogram that will show how open or closed the arteries are. If the blockage is bad, you may be advised to have bypass surgery, in which a blood vessel, usually a vein, is used to bypass the blocked artery in your leg.

What To Do

Nerve damage and vascular problems put you at risk for foot ulcers leading to amputation. Each year, over 80,000 people with diabetes have a toe or part of a foot amputated. *Most* of those amputations could be avoided with preventive care and early treatment of problems. Here's what you can do.

■ See a Foot Doctor
   See a foot doctor soon after your diagnosis of diabetes. He or she will:
   ● Test your feet for loss of protective sensation and poor circulation.
   ● Diagnose and treat athlete's foot.
      Left untreated, this fungal infection

opens the door to further infection.

● Evaluate foot or toe deformities such as hammertoes and bunions.

Foot deformities put you at higher risk of developing a foot ulcer, which may lead to amputation. You'll get advice about padding or special shoes. Your foot doctor may recommend that you have surgery to correct the deformity while you are still young and have good circulation in your feet, so you'll heal quickly after surgery. This can prevent problems in the future.

● Remove corns and calluses.

These put pressure on the tissue underneath. It's like having a stone in your shoe. Ulcers often form under corns and calluses. Your foot doctor will also help you figure out why the corn or callus formed in the first place. It may be because of a deformity, or from poorly fitted shoes. You'll want to solve the problem so corns and calluses don't form again. Special inserts for your shoes, called orthoses, may help.

● Tell you whether you need special shoes or inserts (therapeutic footwear) to help you avoid foot ulcers.

● Talk to you about good foot care.

■ Check Your Shoes

In bare feet, stand on white paper. Have someone trace the outlines of your feet. Now one by one, put every pair of shoes you own on those tracings. Does the outline of either foot stick out beyond the shoe at any point? If so, that shoe is putting pressure on your foot at those places and putting you at risk for a foot ulcer that can lead to amputation. Get rid of those shoes. (A corn or callus is a sign that at least one of your shoes doesn't fit.)

■ Buy Shoes That Fit

● Go to a store with a trained fitter (i.e., not a discount store with a twenty-year-old clerk earning minimum wage). This is to protect you from yourself—if you have neuropathy, you'll tend to choose shoes that are too tight, because you can't feel them. Shoes that fit well may feel too loose to you.

● Have your feet sized every time you buy shoes. Your feet tend to get longer and wider as you grow older. You might be surprised to find out what your size is now. And have both feet sized, as one may be longer than the other.

● Have your feet measured at the end of

the day. Feet often swell during the day, and you want to buy shoes that will fit all day long.

● Keep in mind that sizes vary among different shoe brands and styles. Judge the shoe by how it fits, not the size marked in the shoe.

● Once the shoes are on, there should be ⅜″ to ½″ of space beyond your longest toe while you're standing; at the same time, the ball of your foot should fit well into the widest part of the shoe.

● Walk in the shoes to make sure they fit well. The heels should not slip very much. Don't expect shoes to stretch to fit. If they aren't comfortable at the time of the fitting, don't buy them.

● Check the shoes you're considering against the tracings you made of your feet.

● Wear new shoes an hour or two a day at first. When you take them off, check for any red spots on your feet.

▣ Practice Good Foot Care Every Day

● Have your regular health care provider examine your feet at every visit. When you're waiting in the exam room, take off your shoes and socks.

● Wash, but don't soak, your feet every day. Dry them well, especially between the toes.

- Since you may not feel the discomfort of a developing problem, examine your feet every day. If you can't see the bottoms of your feet, use a mirror or ask someone else (your spouse, your daughter, etc.) to check your feet. At the first sign of a problem—a tiny cut, a blister, a red spot that doesn't fade in half an hour—call your doctor.

- Always wear footwear. Put slippers on even though you're just walking from the bedroom to the bathroom. Wear aqua shoes at the pool and the beach— you never know when you'll step on a sliver of glass. Wear warm, protective shoes when it's very cold out.

- Feel inside your shoes for foreign objects, bumps, and wrinkles. Do this every time before you put them on.

- Wear socks that wick moisture away, such as polyester or a blend. Try to find socks with no seams, or very flat seams.

- Never use heating pads or hot water on your feet. Temperatures that feel only warm to a foot with nerve damage may actually be hot enough to burn.

- Use lotion on your feet. Neuropathy leads to dry skin. Dry skin leads to cracked skin. Cracked skin may lead to an infection. Use a lotion or other moisturizer to keep your skin from getting too dry. (But first have your feet checked by your health care provider to make sure it's simply dry skin and not athlete's foot.) But don't put lotion between your toes. Too much moisture there may lead to problems.

● Don't use over-the-counter corn removers. Don't do "bathroom surgery."

GET MEDICARE TO PAY FOR YOUR SHOES

If you're covered by Medicare Part B and you're at risk for foot ulcers, Medicare will pay for most of the cost of special shoes or inserts that will help prevent foot ulcers that can lead to amputation.

Briefly, to get this benefit, the doctor managing your diabetes care needs to certify that you have one or more of the following conditions that put you at high risk for a foot ulcer:

- partial or complete amputation of the foot
- a foot ulcer in the past
- callus that could lead to a foot ulcer
- nerve damage from diabetes and a problem callus
- foot deformity (for example, hammertoe)
- poor circulation

Go to the Web site of the Pedorthic Footwear
Association at www.pedorthics.org and click on
"Reimbursement." You'll find "Statement Of
Certifying Physician For Therapeutic Shoes,"
which you can print out and give to your diabetes
doctor to fill out, if you qualify.

Then go to a foot doctor (podiatrist) for a prescription for therapeutic footwear. Your foot doctor may decide you need only inserts, or that you
need custom-made shoes. Take the prescription
to a dispenser: a person trained to fit therapeutic
footwear. This could be a podiatrist, orthotist,
prosthetist, or pedorthist.

What Do I Get?
If you qualify, you can get either of the following
each year:

- One pair of depth shoes and three pairs of
  inserts, OR
- One pair of custom-molded shoes (including
  inserts) and two extra pairs of inserts.
  (Custom-molded shoes are covered if you
  have a foot deformity that can't be accommo-
  dated by a depth shoe.)
- Separate inserts may be covered under certain criteria. A shoe modification can be covered as a substitute for an insert.

What Do I Pay?
The Centers for Medicare and Medicaid Services
(CMS) has decided what are reasonable costs for

shoes and orthoses, and Medicare will pay 80% of these costs.

These "allowable costs" were figured with the "average" consumer in mind. You may need more expensive footwear to meet your needs. Medicare still pays only 80% of the allowable cost, not the actual cost of your footwear. Allowable costs increase every year, and they may be different in different states. Recently, the allowable costs were about:

- Depth shoes: $125 per pair
- Custom-molded shoes: $376 per pair
- Inserts or modifications: $64 per pair

If the dispenser you choose "accepts assignment" (agrees to accept the allowable CMS rate), he or she charges you 20% of that rate (plus any deductible) and charges Medicare 80%. To get a list of dispensers that accept assignment, contact your Medicare carrier.

If the dispenser doesn't accept assignment, the charge for the footwear will likely be higher than the allowable cost and you will likely be expected to pay in full, with Medicare reimbursing you for the CMS-allowable amount. When you make the appointment, ask what you'll be expected to pay. Whether the dispenser accepts assignment or not, it's the responsibility of the dispenser to file the paperwork with Medicare.

A description of the shoe benefit is in "Medicare

Coverage of Diabetes Supplies and Services."
Go to www.medicare.gov, click on Publications,
and search for publication number 11022. To
order a hard copy, call 1-800-MEDICARE
(1-800-633-4227).

FORUM

Feet and leg problems

Hi, I am a new member,
female and fifty-two years
old. I was diagnosed about two years ago.
Does anyone else suffer from unbearable
leg tingles, (not just restless leg syndrome). Also recently my feet hurt, top
and bottom, Is this common with diabetes
two? I am so happy to meet all of you and
to have found this site. —C

Re: feet and leg problems
Diagnosed 5 years ago, at 55 years old,
I'm also female, so can really identify
with what you're experiencing. Don't
know if this would help, but when I
started walking every day, my feet
started hurting, and it was that they were
"expanding"; I also switched to heavier
padded socks for my running shoes

(which I quickly switched to from my flimsy Easy Spirit walking shoes and thin socks, and getting larger (longer and wider) and more supportive shoes solved the problem. Now, walking actually helps my feet feel better. Legs, too. If you've recently started a walking program to help control your blood sugar, and your feet feel better when you take off your shoes, this could be part of it. Another thing is that getting the blood sugar down within normal range can sort of "wake up" the nerves, so you maybe now are feeling things you didn't feel before. I hope this helps. —pw

Flu and Pneumonia

Flu: According to the Centers for Disease Control and Prevention, about 10% to 20% of U.S. residents get the flu each year, and an average of 114,000 people are hospitalized for flu-related complications. On average, about 36,000 Americans die per year from the complications of flu.

People with diabetes, especially those with kidney or heart problems, are at high risk for complications, hospitalizations, and death from flu. Therefore, the American Diabetes Association recommends a yearly flu shot for people with diabetes who are 6 months of age or older. You need a shot every year because new flu strains circulate every flu season, so the vaccine is changed each year.

In September, call your doctor's office and say you want a flu shot. You want to get it before the flu season starts, so your body has time to build up immunity. You probably won't need a regular appointment. A nurse can give you the shot. Or call your public health department, senior center, pharmacy, or large grocery store chain that houses pharmacies. They might be holding flu shot clinics.

Flu shots don't give 100% protection, so encourage family members to get flu shots, too, so there's less risk of them giving you the flu.

Pneumonia: People with diabetes are susceptible to developing pneumonia and pneumococcal infections, and they are at higher risk for complications and death from these infections. Risk is higher still for those with diabetes who are 65 or older, and those who have heart, lung, or kidney problems.

The American Diabetes Association recommends you get a one-time pneumonia vaccination. If you got one more than five years ago and you were under 64 years old, and you're now 65 or older, you should get a second pneumonia vaccination. Your doctor may also advise revaccination if you have kidney disease or if you've had an organ transplant.

Sleep Apnea

Are you sleepy during the day? Do you often fall asleep when you're watching T.V. or reading? Have people told you that you snore?

SIGNS AND SYMPTOMS

- You usually snore, and it's loud.
- Someone has seen you actually stop breathing for a few seconds while you're sleeping.
- Your bed partner complains that you kick while you're asleep.
- You're sleepy during the day. You often fall asleep during quiet activities, such as watching T.V. or reading. If you have a severe case, you may even fall asleep while driving, or during conversations or meals.
- You don't think you're sleepy, but you admit you're tired or lack energy during the day.
- Your sleep is restless. You don't wake up refreshed.
- You have awakened choking or gasping.
- When you wake up, you have a sore throat or dry mouth.
- You wake up with a headache.
- You get up during the night to go to the bathroom.
- You often have nighttime esophageal reflux.

RISK FACTORS

- age over 45
- male
- obesity
- neck circumference over 17 inches in men, over 16 inches in women

You may have sleep apnea. You don't breathe normally when you're asleep. It's ruining your sleep now, and it's affecting your health in the long run.

There's growing evidence that sleep apnea raises your risk of having a heart attack or stroke. Because your sleep is disrupted, you're sleepy during the day, and your risk of a car accident or having an accident on the job is higher. You just don't think as well as you would if you were well rested. And when you're practically sleepwalking through your day, you can't exercise, so your diabetes control suffers.

Obesity is a risk factor for both apnea and type 2 diabetes, so many people with diabetes also have sleep apnea. In one study of middle-aged men, 36% of those with diabetes also had sleep apnea, compared with 15% of nondiabetic men.

Diagnosis

Discuss your symptoms with your regular doctor, who may want to send you to an ear, nose, and throat (ENT) specialist. If your insurance allows it, you may want to go right to an ENT. (Look under "otolaryngology.")

The doctor will examine you and determine whether a sleep study—the gold standard for diagnosing sleep apnea—is needed. For a sleep study, you spend a night in a sleep center. Sensors are taped near your eyes, on your chest, on your finger, and on your head. During the night, the technician records whether you stop breathing, for how long and how often, the oxygen saturation of your blood, and what stage of sleep you're in at various times.

Let's say the sleep study shows that you have sleep apnea. What does that mean?

When you lie down, gravity pulls your throat muscles down a bit, which narrows your airway. When you go into a deep sleep, your muscles relax and your airway closes completely. To keep yourself from suffocating, you come up to a lighter level of sleep—or even wake up for a second, though you don't remember it—and breathe.

Then you slip back down into deep sleep, your muscles relax, you start to suffocate, come up again, and on and on it goes. This coming "up" to breathe is called a microarousal. If you have sleep apnea, you may be having hundreds of microarousals every night.

Is it any wonder you feel exhausted after what you thought was a full night's sleep?

What You Can Do On Your Own

▓ Don't drink alcohol or take sedatives
at night. They reduce muscle tone, so
apnea occurs more often. They also delay
arousal, so each apnea episode lasts longer.
▓ Don't get over-tired. Go to bed at a reasonable time.
▓ Lose a little weight. (This will also help
your diabetes and high blood pressure.)
▓ Avoid sleeping on your back. Try this:
Sew a pocket on the back of your pajama
top and put a tennis ball in it. For some
people, this trick keeps them from sleeping on their backs.
▓ Treat year-round or seasonal congestion:
get rid of allergens, use nasal steroids,
decongestants, antihistamines, or saline
washes.

CPAP

Treatment of nasal congestion and lifestyle
changes may work for mild apnea. If your apnea is
moderate or severe, as is true for most people, you
need more aggressive treatment.

The usual first line of therapy is CPAP (contin-
uous positive airway pressure). You are fitted with
a mask that you wear over your nose, or nose and
mouth, while you sleep. It delivers pressurized air,

To lower your risk of these complications:

Do this:	Retinopathy	Nephropathy	Neuropathy	Amputation	Erectile Dysfunction	Heart Attack	Stroke
Lower blood glucose	✓	✓	✓	✓	✓		
Lower blood pressure	✓	✓		✓		✓	✓
Control cholesterol		✓		✓		✓	✓
Quit smoking			✓	✓	✓	✓	✓
Take aspirin						✓	✓

which keeps your airway open.

CPAP therapy is started in a sleep lab, so the technician can adjust the pressure of the air to suit your needs.

Yes, it's intrusive to wear the mask, and it will probably take several weeks to get used to it. But many people report better sleep as soon as they start using it.

Dental Appliances

A dental appliance can be made for you that moves your lower jaw or tongue forward. A recent study showed such appliances were effective in 63% of those with mild to moderate apnea. Again, for more severe apnea, CPAP is the way to go.

Surgery

Surgery that removes part of the soft palate, uvula, and excess tissue in the throat is the most common type of surgery to treat apnea. It's not always successful, and some of the benefit may be lost over time. Long-term side effects, such as difficulty swallowing and nasal regurgitation, have been reported in up to 10% of patients.

New Member of the Club

Hi. I have been newly diagnosed as type 2. This has
just happened in the last
month. My A1C (Gee, I hope I'm pick-
ing up the lingo right!) was 7.5, and my
doctor says that it looks like I'll be able
to control this initially with diet and
exercise. That's something he's been
after me about for a couple of years. I
think it's finally time to listen to him and
do what he says. I already have been in
the hospital with coronary artery disease,
and I have had sleep apnea for years, and
I still haven't done the obvious thing that
I need to do. My wife is very concerned
that I take control of this. (I want very
badly to be an example for her, because
she's right there with me on the weight
issue.) (Don't tell her I said that.) It's
time for me to make a life change.
People say that all the time, and never do
it. Usually, though, they don't die from
it. This is different. I have pulled off a
life change once before, when I quit
smoking cold-turkey. This is going to be
a piece of cake, after that. I promise not

to mention cake again soon. I do look forward to talking to those of you who want to, and getting help from you all. I've always been one of those I-can-do-it-myself people, but it's time to park the ego and get on with it. —wm

Re: New Member of the Club

Let me be the first to welcome you! I'm a newbee too and have 3 stents in my heart from CAD. My doc. has also been suspecting DM for some time, but I kept saying "no, no, no . . . I will not be diabetic too" Tried different diets, etc. . . . but finally had to face it when my A1C was 8.2 and Glucose was 277 (this was a little less than a month ago) . . . so, guess it's yes, yes, yes, I am diabetic! Good job for quitting the cigs . . . I can't seem to let them go altogether . . . and I know that's really bad . . . I'm trying tho'. You have a wonderful attitude about this whole thing and that's what's going to get you through it. This is a great website with great people participating . . . I was so scared at first (you can read my first entry . . .) and now I'm actually writing back to folks and giving advice and encouragement (for what it's worth from someone who's so new to this) . . . Anyway . . . I know you'll get control of this thing . . . keep in touch and good luck. —j2

13

Women

Irregular Periods: PCOS?

Some girls and women with type 2 diabetes have a condition called polycystic ovary syndrome (PCOS), which is related to insulin resistance. They don't ovulate normally. This affects their periods, makes it harder or impossible for them to get pregnant, and may raise their risk of heart disease.

It may seem that if you're having periods, you must be ovulating. That's not necessarily true. In the normal menstrual cycle, female hormones cause the uterus to prepare for a pregnancy, and also cause an egg to mature and be released. When the egg is released (ovulation), the balance of female hormones changes; if the egg is not fertilized, the uterus sheds its lining (your period).

Insulin resistance can lead to an imbalance of female hormones. The uterine lining may build up in the first half of the cycle, but the balance of female hormones isn't right for the release of the egg. Without ovulation, the uterine lining continues to build up. Your period may be late, with heavy flow, clots, and lots of cramps. Or you may have what's called dysfunctional uterine bleeding: You have short "periods" more than once a month, for example bleeding for just two days every two weeks or so.

You may also have too much active testosterone in your system. Normally, women have testosterone, but most of it is not active. With PCOS, it is active. Acne and facial hair are signs of too much active testoterone.

SIGNS AND SYMPTOMS OF PCOS IN TEENS OR ADULT WOMEN

- Abnormal menstrual cycles.
  - No periods
  - Irregular periods
  - Heavy or prolonged bleeding
  - Painful periods
- Can't get pregnant.
- Waist measurement greater than 35 inches, or waist bigger than hips (apple shape).

■ Acanthosis nigricans: Darker patches of skin in neck folds, armpits, folds in waistline, or groin.

■ Facial hair (more hair than is normal for your ethnic group).

■ Acne.

■ Male-pattern hair loss.

To treat PCOS, treat the insulin resistance:

■ Lose some excess weight. Just 5 to 10 pounds will make a difference.

■ Be more physically active.

■ Your doctor may prescribe metformin or a TZD.

Be aware that treatment for PCOS may cause you to start ovulating. Make sure you're using effective birth control until you're ready to get pregnant. Oral contraceptives may be less effective if you use a TZD.

Menstruation

Some women with diabetes notice that their blood glucose levels are higher in the week before their periods or at the start. The reason? The female hormones estrogen and progesterone.

The first day of bleeding is day 1. Around day 13, estrogen levels go up. Ovulation occurs. Then progesterone levels start to go up. Toward the end of the month, if there is no pregnancy, the levels of estrogen and progesterone start to drop and bleeding starts.

Some studies show that when estrogen and progesterone levels are high, you are more insulin resistant. Blood glucose levels creep up. These hormones also cause your liver to release more glucose into your bloodstream. You might eat more just before your period or be less active because of cramps and feeling out-of-sorts. All these raise blood glucose levels.

Are your hormones affecting your blood glucose levels? Look at three months worth of your blood glucose logs. Mark the first day of your period for each month, and look at your blood glucose levels the week before. Were they on average higher (or for some women, lower) than in the other three weeks of the month?

If they're higher, try to be more active the week before your period. This will increase insulin sensitivity. And, as usual, try to watch what you eat. If you use insulin, you may need a little more that week to stay within your blood glucose goals. Talk to your diabetes educator or doctor for guidance on insulin changes.

Birth Control

Effective birth control is extremely important for women and teens who have diabetes, because an unplanned pregnancy in a mother with diabetes means the baby has a higher risk of birth defects.

When the mother's blood glucose level is above the nondiabetic range, there is a higher-than-average risk of birth defects and miscarriage. Many of these problems occur during the first six to eight weeks after conception, when the baby's organs are starting to form, before their mothers even know they're pregnant.

Many mothers-to-be are able to achieve near-normal blood glucose levels, because they know they're doing it for the health of their babies. But very few people with diabetes walk around in their everyday lives with blood glucose levels in the normal range. In addition, other medications women with diabetes often use—for example, statins for lipid control and certain medications for high blood pressure—may affect the fetus.

Therefore, it's very important to use effective birth control until you can plan a pregnancy carefully.

In your younger, wilder days, were you casual about birth control and never got pregnant? Or have you tried to get pregnant in the past and been unable to? Maybe you think you aren't able to get pregnant. That might not be true anymore. You might have had PCOS (see above) and not known it. Many treatments for type 2 diabetes also treat PCOS. You may now be fertile and need birth control.

Your options for birth control are the same as any woman's. The pill, an IUD, a diaphragm plus spermicidal jelly, and condom plus spermicidal foam are all good ways to prevent pregnancy. Sterilization is a choice if you want to prevent pregnancy from ever occurring.

Hormone-based methods include Norplant (implanted contraceptive), Depo-Provera (injected contraceptive), and the pill (oral contraceptive). Before prescribing one of these methods, your doctor will consider your health history and whether you have any diabetes complications. If you choose a hormone-based method, be aware that it might affect your blood glucose levels. Check your blood glucose more often when you first start using the method. Be aware that pioglitazone may reduce the effectiveness of oral contraceptives, so talk to your doctor about using another method.

Consider doubling up on birth control. For example if you use a diaphragm, which can have a failure rate of 18%, have your partner use a condom. This gives you even more protection from pregnancy and some protection from sexually transmitted diseases, including AIDS.

Sex

The fatigue that comes with high blood glucose levels can decrease your desire for sex. High blood glucose levels also increase your risk of yeast infections. So reaching your blood glucose goals may solve some of the problems that make sex less desirable.

Neuropathy can sometimes cause the nerves that supply the genital area to lose feeling. Tighter blood glucose control may help reverse or prevent this. You may also want to try vibrators or other forms of stimulation around the clitoris.

If neuropathy has affected your bladder, causing you to urinate during intercourse or orgasm, empty your bladder before and after sex. This also helps prevent urinary tract infections.

If you're "dry" and intercourse is painful, try an over-the-counter "personal lubricant." In women past menopause, this problem is sometimes treated with estrogen.

If you're on dialysis for end-stage renal disease, you may produce large amounts of the hormone prolactin, which decreases sexual desire. Discuss this with your kidney specialist or doctor.

Pregnancy

For the health of your baby, you'll want blood glucose levels in the normal range when you conceive and throughout your pregnancy. Your baby's organs are formed during the first six to eight weeks after conception. It's critical to have normal blood glucose levels during this time to lower the risk of birth defects. You'll also want normal glucose levels throughout your pregnancy so that there won't be extra glucose making the baby grow too large. In addition, your other medications (for blood pressure, cholesterol, etc.) need to be pregnancy-safe.

Birth defects occur in 6% to 12% of the infants of women with diabetes, compared with 2% to 3% of babies of nondiabetic women. In addition, women with diabetes are more likely to have stillbirths. These risks can be greatly lowered (although not completely removed) with normal blood glucose levels and good care before conception and during pregnancy and delivery.

Plasma Glucose Goals at Conception and During Pregnancy

	Goal
Before meals	80–110 mg/dl
2 hours after meals	less than 155 mg/dl
A1C	In the normal range. (Normal range depends on which test is done. A common normal range is under 6%.)

Plan Your Pregnancy

Three to six months before you try to conceive, tell your health care provider that you want to get pregnant.

If you aren't seeing a diabetes specialist now, your doctor may want to refer you to one.

Diabetes pills have not been proven safe to use during pregnancy. If you use diabetes pills now, your doctor will want to start you on insulin. You'll need more insulin as the pregnancy progresses.

Get a thorough physical exam by your doctor before you become pregnant. Your doctor will be looking for any health problems that could endanger your health or your baby's.

If you've had diabetes for more than 10 years and you have other risk factors for heart disease, your doctor may want you to have tests to check your heart's health.

Your doctor should look for signs of damage to nerves (neuropathy) that control things such as heart rate and blood vessel opening and narrowing. This diabetes complication can affect how your heart and blood pressure will react to the physical stress of pregnancy.

Your prepregnancy exam should include tests for kidney function. In some women, kidney disease gets worse during pregnancy. If you have impaired kidney function, you should know pregnancy may be more difficult for you to manage and you may be troubled by edema (swelling) and high blood pressure.

See an eye doctor for a dilated eye exam. Eye disease should be treated before you become pregnant. Diabetic retinopathy may develop or get worse during pregnancy. It can be treated during pregnancy, so continue to have eye exams during pregnancy. Retinopathy tends to return to its prepregnancy level after delivery.

In addition, your doctor should take a blood sample to measure your thyroid function and your A1C.

If you smoke, quit. If you drink alcohol, stop.

Your Medical Team

The ideal health care team for your pregnancy includes:

- A doctor who is a specialist in diabetes.
- An obstetrician with experience in high-risk pregnancies.
- A dietitian. Meal planning will take on a high priority. It's worth it to pay a special visit to your dietitian to get help making dietary changes to meet the demands of pregnancy. You may need strategies for dealing with morning sickness.
- A diabetes educator.
- A pediatrician interested in the care of infants of mothers with diabetes.

After Delivery

After delivery, if you haven't gained too much

weight, you'll probably be able to go back to taking an oral agent, unless you're breastfeeding.

Some overweight women find they can stick to their meal plans during pregnancy like they never could before. (A baby is a great motivator.) They manage to weigh less after delivery than before they got pregnant, and they need less or no diabetes medication after delivery.

Breast milk is the ideal food for a new baby. If you haven't considered breastfeeding, gather information during your pregnancy so you can make an informed choice.

"I WAS NOT PLANNING ON IT."

Pamé Moore-Barr went in for her annual exam and found out she was pregnant.

"I was not planning on it, not even thinking about having another child," she says. Her doctor referred her to an endocrinologist, who took Moore-Barr off the oral agent she'd been taking and started her on insulin.

"Having to stick myself four times a day for insulin, and then four times a day to check my blood sugars—I really didn't want to deal with that. But I wanted a healthy baby, so I had to do it."

Moore-Barr weighed over 250 pounds going into the pregnancy, but then made big changes: no sodas, no chocolate, no cheesecake. "During my pregnancy, I was truly the best I could be," she says.

Her A1C was 7% in the beginning of her pregnancy and stayed around 6% throughout.

Moore-Barr had a healthy baby boy. "I'm truly happy I followed my doctor's orders."

Kids with Type 2

"Used to be." You'll hear that a lot about diabetes.

Type 2 diabetes used to be called adult-onset diabetes. Most cases were diagnosed in people over age 40. Now more and more children and teens are being diagnosed with type 2 diabetes.

Type 2 diabetes used be thought of as a milder form of diabetes. Years ago, before diabetes care got better, many people who developed type 1 diabetes as children had long-term complications of diabetes 10 or 20 years later, in what should have been the prime of their lives.

In contrast, people were most often diagnosed with type 2 diabetes in their fifties or sixties. Many died of heart attacks before kidney disease or vision loss had been detected. And the premature heart attacks weren't linked with diabetes back then. So type 2 diabetes just didn't seem as serious.

But now kids are developing type 2 diabetes. They often have high blood pressure and unhealthy lipid levels as well, which further raises their risk of diabetes complications. Without aggressive treatment, in 10 or 20 years many may have kidney damage, neuropathy, and cardiovascular disease.

Diagnosis

A 12-year-old child has high blood sugar. Is it type 1 or type 2 diabetes? It's not always clear.

Insulin needs go up with puberty, probably because of the increase in growth hormone during that time. Insulin needs go back down when puberty is complete. This is true in all children, whether they have diabetes or not.

A child who is developing type 1 diabetes is losing a lot of the cells that produce insulin. The increased demand for insulin during adolescence is too much for the few remaining insulin-producing cells. Blood sugars go up, and diabetes is diagnosed. The most common age for diagnosis of type 1 diabetes is 10 to 12 years old in girls and 12 to 14 years old in boys.

Most children who develop type 2 diabetes are diagnosed during puberty as well. In a child who is already insulin resistant, puberty is sometimes enough to tip the scales to type 2 diabetes.

Signs and symptoms at diagnosis can also overlap. Many children with type 1 diabetes have diabetic ketoacidosis at diagnosis. Adults with type 2 rarely have DKA at diagnosis. Yet many children with type 2, like those with type 1, have DKA at diagnosis.

So diagnosing a child with high blood sugars as having type 1 or type 2 diabetes can be tricky. Still, there are risk factors and signs that tip the diagnosis toward type 2.

RISK FACTORS AND SIGNS OF TYPE 2 IN CHILDREN

- Overweight: 85% are overweight at diagnosis (Body Mass Index over 27, or over the 85th percentile for age and sex.)
- Family history of type 2 diabetes: Most have a first- or second-degree relative with type 2 diabetes (though the adults may be diagnosed after the child).
- Acanthosis nigricans: In darker-skinned children, darker patches of skin in neck folds (it looks like the neck folds are dirty), armpits, folds in waistline, or groin. This is a sign of insulin resistance. It's often seen in children with insulin resistance but not usually seen in adults.
- Non-European decent: African American, Hispanic, Asian American, American Indian, Pacific Islander.

- In girls, irregular periods or other signs of polycystic ovary syndrome.
- High blood pressure and high cholesterol (metabolic syndrome).
- Age 10 or over. Most are in middle to late puberty. But now that American children grow overweight and inactive at ever younger ages, younger children—5 to 10 years old—are being diagnosed with type 2 diabetes.

Usually, the signs, symptoms, and risk factors will allow the doctor to tell whether it's type 1 or type 2. The doctor should order blood tests to be sure. Children with type 1 will have antibodies in their blood that show that their bodies are attacking their own insulin-producing cells. They also have a very low level of natural insulin. Children with type 2 will have much higher levels of insulin (but because of insulin resistance, it's not enough to keep blood sugars down), and none of the antibodies associated with type 1.

Most children diagnosed with diabetes have either type 1 or type 2. There is another, less common, type called **atypical diabetes,** seen in African American children. These children don't have the antibodies of type 1 diabetes. They typically aren't obese, and they don't have acanthosis nigricans or other signs of insulin resistance. Family members in several generations have been diagnosed with diabetes before age 40.

GROWTH CHARTS

Body mass index (BMI) is a ratio of weight to height. It gives a better assessment of who is overweight than simple height/weight charts. In children, percentiles for BMI are specific to the child's age and sex.

Take your child's weight in pounds, divide by height in inches, divide by height again, then multiply by 703. That's his or her BMI. Find your child's age on the bottom of the chart on pp. 282, 283 (for boys) or pp. 284, 285 (for girls). Draw a vertical line up from your child's age. Draw a horizontal line across from his or her BMI. See where the lines intersect, and check the percentile lines.

To print out a chart to keep with your child's records, go to: www.cdc.gov/growthcharts. Click on "Clinical Growth Charts." Page down and click on "Set 1," page down to "Children 2 – 20 (5th – 95th percentile)," page down to either "Boys BMI-for-age" or "Girls BMI-for-age."

Treatment

As in adults, treatment for type 2 in children addresses the ABCs.

■ **A1C** (average blood sugar)

The goal is near-normal blood glucose levels, reflected by an A1C of less than 7%. Most chil-

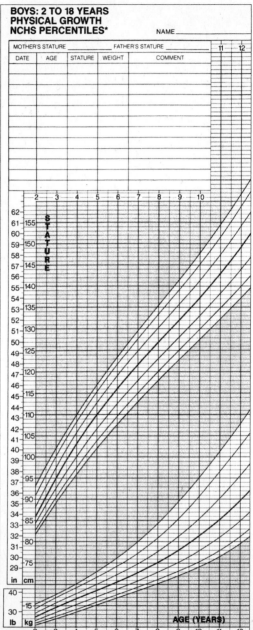

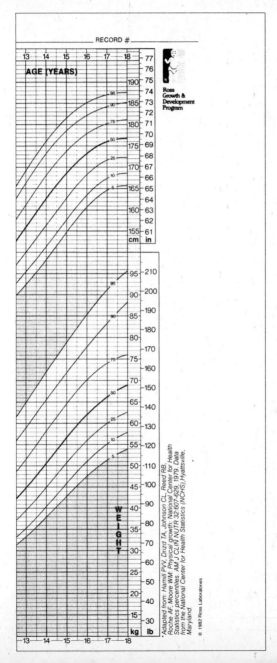

GIRLS: 2 TO 18 YEARS
PHYSICAL GROWTH
NCHS PERCENTILES*

NAME _____

MOTHER'S STATURE _____	FATHER'S STATURE _____			
DATE	AGE	STATURE	WEIGHT	COMMENT

STATURE

in | cm

lb | kg

AGE (YEA

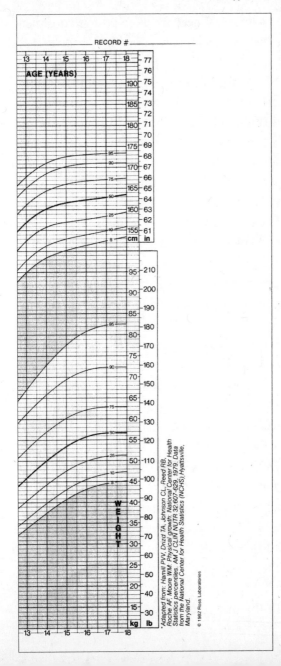

Adapted from: Hamill PVV, Drizd TA, Johnson CL, Reed RB, Roche AF, Moore WM. Physical growth: National Center for Health Statistics percentiles. AM J CLIN NUTR 32:607-629, 1979. Data from the National Center for Health Statistics (NCHS), Hyattsville, Maryland.

© 1982 Ross Laboratories

dren with type 2 need the three-pronged treatment plan to reach their goals.

Medical Nutrition Therapy: Find a registered dietitian with experience with children and diabetes. Goals depend on your child's age. For younger children with type 2, the goal might be to stop or slow down weight gain as he or she keeps growing taller. Older teens may have a goal of weight loss.

Have all caregivers go to the sessions. Help your whole family change their eating habits. For one thing, you don't want your child to feel as though he or she is being singled out and punished by having, say, soda and junk food taken away. Two, the fact that one child has been diagnosed means that diabetes is in your family's genes. All your family members—adults and children—are at above-average risk for developing diabetes. Losing a little weight and being more active can prevent type 2 diabetes in other family members. (See Chapter 15.)

Help your children to eat only when they're hungry, not when they're simply bored or, like, totally stressed about something that happened at school. Model other ways of dealing with stress. Say to your child, "I had a terrible day at work. I need a walk. Come with me and tell me about your day."

In the past, did you reward your child with

food? Now, think of activity-related rewards. If your child brings home a good report card, get a water-bottle holder for her bike, buy him a kite, or take the whole family to play miniature golf.

Physical activity: Again, you don't want your child to feel punished by being made to "exercise" for a certain number of minutes a day while everyone else sits around. Your whole family will benefit from active activities. Walk or bike to school, parks, the library, and playgrounds. If these places are truly too far or too unsafe to walk or bike to, park your car a few blocks away and walk the rest of the way. A two- or three-block walk every day will do a lot for your child's blood glucose, blood pressure, and lipid levels. (Yours, too!)

See if your child would like to sign up for a team sport. If he or she doesn't feel able to keep up or fears being teased, suggest individual sports such as swimming, karate, or horseback riding lessons.

Reduce screen time—TV, movies, computer games or chat groups—to less than two hours a day. Besides the fact that these are slug activities, TV ads for food will make your child want to eat. Consider having your child earn screen time with exercise. For example, a swim lesson or biking to school earns 15 minutes of screen time.

Consider an after-school program. Try to find one that schedules physical activity, either outdoor or indoor. Even an after-school class that doesn't involve physical activity will be better than your child coming home and snacking in front of the TV until the adults get home from work.

Boys and girls who watch four or more hours of television each day had greater body fat and had a greater body mass index than those who watched less than two hours per day.
–Third National Health and Nutrition Examination Survey, *JAMA* 1998;279:938–942

Medication: Most children with type 2 are prescribed metformin, which is approved for use in children ages 10 and up. Metformin may help with weight loss, and it may lower triglyceride and LDL levels. Note that people who binge drink should not use metformin.

Some doctors prescribe other oral agents for children and get good results.

Children who are very ill at the time of diagnosis may need insulin at first. After the very high blood sugars come down, the child will probably be prescribed an oral agent, and insulin doses will slowly be reduced until the child is using only an oral agent, MNT therapy, and physical activity to control his or her diabetes. Over time, weight loss and increased physical activity could help to reduce or eliminate the need for oral medications, too.

Blood Pressure

The goal is a blood pressure that is normal for your child's age and sex. Losing some excess weight, quitting tobacco (more than a third of high school students use tobacco products), and being more active is usually enough to reduce blood pressure.

If not, then medication may be needed. The choices are the same as for adults.

Cholesterol

Although it may seem alarmist to talk about cardiovascular disease in children, that's when it starts. Unhealthy levels of lipids (cholesterol) means artery-clogging plaque is forming in your child's arteries. Lipid control is as important as it is in adults.

A fasting lipid profile, a blood test showing the levels of various blood fats, is in order. The American Diabetes Association recommends the following for children with type 2 diabetes:

■ Have a fasting lipid profile done shortly after the diagnosis of diabetes, but after blood glucose levels have come under control. (Just lowering blood glucose may improve lipids.)

■ If normal, repeat the profile every two years.

Lipid Goals for Children and Adolescents with Diabetes

Type of Lipid	Goal
LDL ("bad") cholesterol	under 100 mg/dl
HDL ("good") cholesterol	over 35 mg/dl
Triglycerides	under 150 mg/dl

Children with type 2 diabetes often have high triglycerides, normal or slightly high LDL, and low HDL, the same pattern seen in adults with type 2. The first steps to lower lipid levels are:

- Get good blood glucose control using diet, physical activity, and medication if needed. Triglycerides often come down as blood sugars come down.
- Lose some excess weight and be more active. This may help raise HDL.
- Use MNT therapy to lower LDL. If your family is seeing a dietitian for help with blood glucose control or weight loss, you're ahead of the game. Your dietitian has probably already recommended a diet that will help lower cholesterol. It's the same as the diet for adults with high cholesterol.

Repeat Profile: Lipid profiles should be done again at three and six months. If despite diet therapy, weight loss, and better blood glucose control, your child's lipid levels are still above goal, the ADA recommends the following:

If LDL level is 100–129 mg/dl: Keep working at blood glucose control, weight loss, and diet therapy. If you haven't seen a dietitian yet, see one now. It's not easy to change the family's habits. Get professional help. Diet therapy will help your child—and the rest of your family—reach blood glucose, weight, blood pressure, and lipid goals.

If LDL level is 130–159 mg/dl: If your child is over 10 years old, your doctor may consider medication. He or she will base the decision on your child's cardiovascular disease risk profile. This includes the levels of other lipids, blood pressure, whether your child smokes, and the family history of cardiovascular disease. For example, a parent who had a heart attack before age 55 is a red flag.

If LDL level is 160 mg/dl or over: Begin medication.

Medication to Lower LDL

Your child's doctor may first try one of the bile acid binders, also known as resins. These medications act like soluble fiber—they lower cholesterol by binding bile acids in the small intestine.

Advantages: These drugs are not absorbed into

the bloodstream, so they don't cause systemic (throughout the body) effects. These medications have been shown to be safe to use in children.

Disadvantages: Gastrointestinal side effects including gas, constipation, upset stomach, and heartburn are frequent. Another disadvantage is that some come as powders. You mix a packet of powder in a small glass of water and drink it down. Some resins come as tablets, but your child may have to take several at a time. All in all, your child or teen may say, "No way."

So your doctor may consider a statin. These have been shown to be safe and effective in teens.

Like adults, your child will need blood tests periodically to be sure the liver can tolerate the medication. If your child complains of significant muscle pain or soreness, report this to the doctor right away.

If your daughter is sexually active, her doctor may not want to risk prescribing a statin. If used during pregnancy, statins may cause birth defects. If your daughter is prescribed a statin, arrange for her to talk to a health care professional about effective birth control.

Triglycerides: If your child's triglyceride level is 150 mg/dl or higher, redouble efforts at getting blood glucose levels down and losing excess weight. Triglycerides often come down when blood glucose levels come down.

If triglycerides are 1,000 mg/dl or higher, your child is at risk of developing pancreatitis, and your doctor will consider using medication.

Beyond the ABCs

Smoking

Preach against smoking loudly and often. If you smoke, quit as an example.

Pregnancy Counseling

Girls with type 2 diabetes may also have polycystic ovary syndrome. Treatment may cause your daughter to start ovulating, and she may be at risk for pregnancy.

Have your daughter talk with a health care professional about effective birth control. The risk of birth defects is higher than average when the mother's A1C is over 6%, when she is on an oral agent for diabetes, or when she is taking certain blood pressure or lipid-lowering medications.

Watch for Depression

Children who are overweight or obese are often teased by peers, which can lead to depression and low self-esteem. Consider mental health counseling for your child.

Sleep Apnea

This is very common in people who are obese. Watch for signs in your child. A child who isn't sleeping well because of sleep apnea may be inattentive in school and may be misdiagnosed as having attention deficit disorder.

Screening for Diabetes Complications
Dilated eye exam: Yearly starting at diagnosis
Test for microalbuminuria: Yearly starting at
     diagnosis

Schools must re-institute vigorous physical education programs for all children and in all grades.

The selling of candy and sugar-containing drinks in schools must be forbidden. Fast foods loaded with calories and fat must not be available in school settings. We must put the health and welfare of our children above the financial benefits accrued by selling junk food in school.

Our communities need to develop safe locations for children and their families to exercise. After-school programs need to include physical activities and provide good nutrition.

We are in the midst of an epidemic. There is a role for each of us in helping to put an end to the rise of this devastating disease in children.

Francine Ratner Kaufman, MD
Clinical Diabetes 20:217–218, 2002

Web sites that promote walking to school:

www.walktoschool.org

www.iwalktoschool.org

Your child is more likely to start smoking if he or she sees characters in movies smoking. Smoke Free Movies (University of California, San Francisco), has a simple solution: Give an "R" rating to movies that show smoking. For more information on the problem and solutions, go to: smokefreemovies.ucsf.edu.

15

Saving Your Family: Prevention of Type 2 Diabetes

If only . . .

If only you had been tested for diabetes earlier. You wouldn't have had untreated diabetes for two or six or ten years—years of high blood sugars that made you feel tired and laid the groundwork for complications.

If only you had known what to do to prevent or delay diabetes. It could have meant many more years of good health.

Don't let your hard-earned hindsight go to waste.

Anyone related to you by blood shares some of your genetic background and has a higher-than-average risk of developing type 2 diabetes. Friends who are overweight or who have other risk factors are also at higher-than-average risk. You can do two things to help your family members and friends:

1) If they have diabetes but don't know it, you'll do them a world of good by helping them get diagnosed. Have them take the Risk Test below.

2) We now know that type 2 diabetes can be delayed or even prevented. Show your loved ones the way.

Could you have diabetes and not know it? Take this risk test.

	If yes:
My weight is equal to or above that listed in the chart on p. 299.	5 pts
I am under 65 years of age *and* I get little or no exercise during a usual day.	5 pts
I am between 45 and 64 years of age.	5 pts
I am 65 years old or older.	9 pts
I am a woman who has had a baby weighing more than 9 pounds at birth.	1 pt
I have a sister or brother with diabetes.	1 pt
I have a parent with diabetes.	1 pt
Total Points:	

Scoring

3–9 points:
You are probably at low risk for having diabetes now. But don't just forget about it—especially if you are Hispanic/Latino, African American, American Indian, Asian American, or Pacific Islander. You may be at higher risk in the future.

10 or more points:
You are at greater risk for having diabetes. Only your health care provider can determine if you have diabetes. At your next office visit, find out for sure.

At-Risk Weight Chart

Height (ft/in) no shoes	Weight (lb) no clothing	Height (ft/in) no shoes	Weight (lb) no clothing
4'10"	129	5'8"	177
4'11"	133	5'9"	182
5'0"	138	5'10"	188
5'1"	143	5'11"	193
5'2"	147	6'0"	199
5'3"	152	6'1"	204
5'4"	157	6'2"	210
5'5"	162	6'3"	216
5'6"	167	6'4"	221
5'7"	172		

Ask your doctor if you need to be tested for diabetes, which is usually done with a fasting blood glucose test. The American Diabetes Association suggests testing every three years beginning at age 45, particularly in those with a body mass index of 25 or higher. (See BMI chart.)

Testing for type 2 diabetes in high-risk children should begin at age 10, or at onset of puberty if puberty occurs before age 10, and should be done every two years. Children at high risk are those who are overweight, with a BMI greater than 85th percentile for age and sex (see pp. 282–285), *plus* have any two of the following risk factors:

- Family history of type 2 diabetes (parents, siblings, grandparents, aunts, uncles)
- Native American, African-American, Latino, Asian-American, Pacific Islander
- Signs of insulin resistance: acanthosis nigricans, high blood pressure, high cholesterol, polycystic ovary syndrome

Prevention

You know about impaired glucose tolerance (IGT, p. 5). Over time, some people with IGT will get better and go back to normal glucose tolerance, some will still have IGT, and some will get worse and move on to diabetes.

The Diabetes Prevention Program, sponsored by the National Institutes of Health, enrolled 3,234 adults with IGT. The participants were split into three groups so the researchers could test three different treatments. They wanted to see if one of the treatments would keep more people from developing type 2 diabetes.

Two groups got standard advice about making their lifestyles healthier. They were advised to eat a healthy diet (less than 30% of calories from fat, less than 10% of calories from saturated fat, less than 300mg dietary cholesterol), to lose some excess weight, and to be more active. They got this information in printed handouts and during a yearly appointment with a health care provider.

The people in one of those groups also took metformin every day. The people in the other group took placebo pills: pills that looked like the metformin pills but contained no drug.

The third group received intensive lifestyle counseling. During the first six months of the study, each took 16 classes to learn how to switch to healthy, low-calorie, low-fat diets and to work up to 150 minutes a week (20 to 30 minutes on most days) of moderate exercise, such as brisk walking. After that, they met once a month or so with case managers to help them keep up their new, healthy lifestyles. The goal for the people in this group was to lose 7% of body weight (a 200-pound person would aim to lose 14 pounds). After six months, 50% had reached their weight loss goal.

The researchers tested glucose tolerance in all participants every year. Participants were followed for up to five years. After one year, 25% of people in the placebo group had gone back to normal glucose tolerance, and 13% had gotten worse and been diagnosed with diabetes. The metformin group was a little bit better: 29% had gone back to normal glucose tolerance, and only 8% had moved on to diabetes. The intensive lifestyle group did the best: over 44% went back to normal, and only 4% moved on to diabetes.

What does this mean for your relatives? The researchers estimate that after three years of an intensive diet and exercise program such as the one used in DPP, only 14% of people with IGT will develop diabetes, compared with 29% of people with IGT given standard advice alone.

What You Can Do

You're already eating a healthier diet and getting more active. These help you lower your blood sugars, blood pressure, and cholesterol. Now you know that this healthier lifestyle will help your loved ones delay or even prevent diabetes. So invite (demand, insist, nag) your family to join you. While you help yourself, you'll help your friends and family keep one step ahead of diabetes.

■ Don't let them call it "your diabetic diet." It's your family's new, healthy way of eating.

- Invite your spouse or a friend to join you for your evening walk.
- Drag your kids along on your bike rides and walks.
- Refuse to drive your children everywhere. If your children are too young to go alone, walk or bike with them.
- Protest any cuts of recess or P.E. time at your children's schools.
- Decree one day a month—for example, the first of the month, or the first Sunday—a screen-free day: no TV, computer games, or videos.

FORUM

Lack of support

I have a question that some of you must have encountered. My husband is not very supportive about this DM thing. He's sorry I have it, but just can't seem to understand the lifestyle changes I have to make. He doesn't understand my diet at all, and seems to think there's nothing wrong with a blood sugar of 150. He says I have become 'obsessive' about food, diet, and checking my BS. He says, "you're no different now than you were over the past couple of years, and you probably had it then" (and, I probably did . . . but I also felt lousy most of the time). I can do this with or without his support, but it would be a lot easier with it. Any good publications out there aimed toward family members? Thanks guys for all your help over the past couple of weeks since I found this site. —j2

Re: Lack of support
It's hard to understand men sometimes. Maybe he's just trying to reassure you in his own way, or he might be very concerned about you. You might want to point out to your husband that you are going to be better than ever, and he is also going to be the beneficiary of your new way of cooking in addition to your own improved health, from which he will benefit indirectly. My husband was 70 pounds overweight, and he lost it within the same first 6 months after my diagnosis 5 years ago when I lost my 40 pounds. Both of us lost 23% of our body weight, and have kept it off with healthier eating and increased activity levels. (I joke that I don't know if he was trying to keep up with me or outdo me! We actually had to stagger our treadmill schedule for the first year, then he tapered off, but I'm still at it.) Speaking of activity, and Peg's post reminds me of

another thing you can do with a cookbook or two: use them for tricep extensions and overhead presses. You will build lean muscle mass, which will help soak up some of the blood sugar. —pw

Re: Lack of support

Boy did this start a discussion! Obviously a pretty common problem. I didn't intend to make my husband out to be a bad guy . . . it's just that he is like many people who don't understand how really dangerous DM can be. He thinks he knows, but he hasn't got a clue. He eats what I put in front of him and lately it has been good, healthy food . . . he doesn't need to lose wt., but has dropped 3 pounds in spite of himself . . . Also, he's trying to keep up with me in the exercise department just to prove he can . . . He has heart problems, and the exercise is a good thing for him. The biggest problem is that he keeps offering me stuff . . . like candy bars and ice cream . . . drives me nuts. Unfortunately, this tells me that he really doesn't understand it yet. YES . . . HE HAS A STRONG FAMILY HISTORY OF DM . . . so the more he can learn the better off he will be too. . . . Thanks to so many of you who responded . . . —j2

This Year

Test	How Often?	Goal	Date/Result	Date/Result	Date/Result	Date/Result
A1C	4x/year (2x/year if goals are reached and control is stable)	Under 7%				
Blood pressure	Every routine health care visit	Under 130/80				
LDL	1x/year if meeting goals	Less than 100				
HDL	1x/year if meeting goals	Over 40				
Triglycerides	1x/year if meeting goals	Less than 150				
Monofilament testing of feet	1x/year			--	--	--
Microalbuminuria	1x/year	Less than 30		--	--	--
Flu shot	1x/year			--	--	--
Pneumonia shot	Once			--	--	--